# Vaughan Williams Symphonies

*Hugh Ottaway*

HUGH OTTAWAY

# VAUGHAN WILLIAMS

*Symphonies*

BBC MUSIC GUIDES

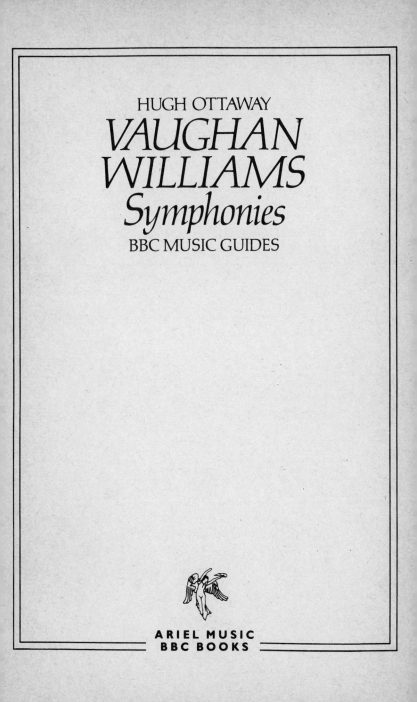

**ARIEL MUSIC**
**BBC BOOKS**

*To Jane*

The principles which govern the composition of music . . . are not the tricks of the trade or even the mysteries of the craft, they are founded on the very nature of human beings.

*Vaughan Williams*

The music examples are reproduced by the kind permission of the following: Faber Music Ltd on behalf of J. Curwen and Sons Ltd for the *Pastoral Symphony* (Ex. 11-14); Stainer and Bell Ltd for *A Sea Symphony* (© 1926, Ex. 2-6), and *A London Symphony* (© 1920, Ex. 1, 7-10); Oxford University Press for Symphonies No. 4 (© 1935, Ex. 15-19), No. 5 (© 1946, Ex. 20-3), No. 6 (© 1950, Ex 24-7), *Sinfonia Antartica* (© 1953, Ex. 28, 30-2), No. 8 (© 1956, Ex. 33-5), No. 9 (© 1958, Ex. 29, 36-9).

Published by BBC Books
A division of BBC Enterprises Ltd
35 Marylebone High Street, London WIM 4AA

ISBN 0 563 20557 1

First published 1972
Reprinted 1977, 1980, 1987

© Hugh Ottaway 1972

Printed in England by Mackays of Chatham Ltd

# Introduction

The English symphony is almost entirely a twentieth-century creation. When in 1903 Vaughan Williams began to sketch the songs for chorus and orchestra that became *A Sea Symphony*, Elgar had not yet emerged as a symphonist. And, extraordinary though it may seem, Elgar's First (1908) is the earliest symphony by an English composer in the permanent repertory. Its stature was recognised at once and the hundredth performance came in little more than a year, a record approached (not equalled) only by Vaughan Williams's Sixth, just forty years later. By the time Vaughan Williams had completed his Ninth – in 1958, a few months before his death at the age of eighty-five – the English symphony as represented by such different composers as Vaughan Williams himself, Bax, Walton, Rubbra and Tippett, not to mention lesser figures, had become a central feature of our musical revival. To say that Vaughan Williams played a major part in bringing this about is to state the obvious: throughout much of the period he was actively involved in English musical life, not only as a composer but as teacher, conductor, organiser and, increasingly, adviser to younger men. Each of his symphonies, from the *London* to the *Antartica* (Nos. 2–7), made a lasting impression; each created its own imaginative world and was felt to mark a new stage in the composer's inner development. Apart from the *Antartica,* which is a special case, none could conceivably have been predicted. When the Eighth and Ninth appeared, the musical climate was changing; both works were underrated, and the significance of the Ninth was very largely missed.

At the deepest level, Vaughan Williams was an intuitive artist, visionary and non-intellectual; a poet in sound whose perceptions, however complex, can usually be referred to one or other of his basic responses to experience. The only aspect of music he was disposed to theorise about was human and social, not technical:

> ... art, like charity, should begin at home. If it is to be of any value it must grow out of the very life of [the artist] himself, the community in which he lives, the nation to which he belongs. [And again:] The composer must not shut himself up and think about art, he must live with his fellows and make his art an expression of the whole life of the community – if we seek for art we shall not find it.

But when he argued these views – in, for instance, *Who wants the*

*English Composer?* (1912) and *National Music* (1934) – he was not so much theorising as advocating a practice which both intuition and common sense told him was the right one.

Common sense was the level most apparent to all who encountered him in practical music-making. Together with his very real loathing of pretentious artiness – what he called 'being exquisite' – and the 'serviceable' nature of many of his smaller compositions, this tended to foster the image of a plain, blunt Englishman, stolid through and through. It may be that he liked that image, partly because there was an element of truth in it – truth about the man in his day-to-day relationships – and partly as a defence, a protection for the artist within. The intuitive artist is always highly vulnerable. Vaughan Williams was no exception; he was far more intense and inwardly aflame than was generally recognised, even by those with a deep appreciation of his music. His enraged outbursts, though proverbial, were seldom seen as the pointers they were. Once, as a young man, he lay awake all night after Mahler's performance of *Tristan und Isolde*: a remarkably Mahler-like reaction, which is worth keeping in mind. The nervous intensity and excitability is there in his music. It is a potent factor even in works whose essential spirit might seem to be one of single-minded contemplation and 'stability'. Think of the climax of the Tallis Fantasia, or the sudden impassioned declamation in the finale of the *Pastoral Symphony*, or the great eruption of the strings in the Preludio of the Fifth. . . . And in all such instances the tone is visionary.

This is not an attempt to turn Vaughan Williams into a late-romantic, though he did in fact belong to that generation. (He was born in 1872, the same year as Skryabin!) What he inherited from the nineteenth century was not the romantic agony; it was a view of the symphony and an almost religious valuation of the artist's vision. These he transformed, but the roots are there. Despite resistances, notably in the official biographies,[1] the idea persists that Vaughan Williams's symphonies are 'about' something: not about London, or the sea, or Antarctica – these are externals, in a way incidentals – but something to do with the composer's perception of reality. This needs very careful handling. The resistances were brought into play by critics who insisted that one symphony

[1] Ursula Vaughan Williams, *R.V.W.* (Oxford, 1964) and Michael Kennedy, *The Works of Ralph Vaughan Williams* (Oxford, 1964).

'meant' war, another peace – and so on. It has even been alleged that all except the Eighth are programme symphonies. That, however, is another question; a programme, properly speaking, is a conscious device, whereas the kind of perception which pervades the best music of Vaughan Williams springs from well below the conscious level.

It is perfectly understandable that in the 1940s and 1950s this music was often spoken of in terms of prophecy or of a spiritual quest. One of the troubles with that approach is its latent sentimentality: the composer himself, that 'extraordinary ordinary man' (Michael Kennedy), was driven to writing facetious programme-notes largely, I suspect, by a desire to counter the prophetic sentimentalists. But the main objection is to the way in which the 'spiritual journeying' school blurs and distorts the tensions and conflicts *within* Vaughan Williams's vision of reality. Far better to see each of the symphonies up to the *Antartica* as an exploration in a different direction than to make too close an analogy with Bunyan and *The Pilgrim's Progress*. Perhaps we should remind ourselves that the symphony with definite Bunyan associations is the Fifth, and that its modal-diatonic assurances, shattered in the Sixth, do not reappear in the last three symphonies. There we find a tragic but resilient humanism, which is the prevailing temper of Vaughan Williams's final period.

A less inhibited understanding of the tensions and conflicts is long overdue. 'He was an atheist during his later years at Charterhouse and at Cambridge, though he later drifted into a cheerful agnosticism: he was never a professing Christian.' Thus Ursula Vaughan Williams, without further comment.[1] Surely the crucial point is that Vaughan Williams, like Thomas Hardy, was a first-generation atheist with a deep attachment to the past, which means a disappointed theist. The implications are immense, and the comparison with Hardy is poignantly underlined by 'The Oxen', the one poem of his that Vaughan Williams set to music.[2] One thinks, too, of Hardy's feeling for southern England, for the land and its people and all that has made them what they are, a feeling at once elegiac and quietly sustaining; above all, perhaps, one thinks of his compassion in the face of life's tragedy, and of the grandeur of his imagination – or rather, the decidedly Vaughan Williams-like

[1] *Op. cit.*
[2] No. 7 in the Christmas Cantata, *Hodie*.

blend of grandeur and intimacy, cosmic visioning and homely lyricism. The temptation to pursue this further is a strong one, for these two artists had so much in common, in qualities of style no less than in their human responses. Vaughan Williams's reverence for folk-song as the musical currency of generations of Englishmen – nameless men with whom he felt a deep, contemplative sympathy – his love of the modes and his delight in archaic expression generally, these have obvious parallels in the work of Hardy. But such a comparison has a place here only if it helps us to understand how a man whose mind rejected Christian *theology* could be profoundly moved by the Christian *tradition* as an embodiment of human hopes and aspirations. And if our understanding is to bear upon the symphonies, it must have some insight into the fundamental tension in Vaughan Williams's work: that between inherited concepts of belief and morality as epitomised in the Fifth and the spiritual desolation which has its loneliest expression in the Epilogue of the Sixth.

The symphonies were written at fairly regular intervals throughout the composer's life, but with gathering speed towards the end. The relatively close succession in which the last three appeared undoubtedly reflects their broadly similar orientation. These three will always be grouped together. The others, too, are usually grouped in threes, though not primarily because Nos. 1–3 have descriptive titles, Nos. 4–6 only their keys. Musically, the main distinction between the earlier and the middle symphonies must turn on the latter's greater concentration and absorption of their material, which means that the *Pastoral* (No. 3) has a fair claim to be associated with them. On balance, however, it seems best to use the familiar grouping.

In the following chronology the details immediately below each title refer to the first performance: date, promoter and venue, conductor. Small revisions of a purely practical nature, such as those made in the scoring of the *Pastoral* as late as 1950, are not noted.

> 1903–9   *A Sea Symphony*
>          1910, Leeds Festival – Vaughan Williams
>          Revised down to 1923
> 1912–13  *A London Symphony*
>          1914, F. B. Ellis, London – Toye
>          Revised 1918, 1920 and 1933

?–1921    *Pastoral Symphony*
          1922, Royal Phil. Soc., London – Boult
1931–4    Symphony [No. 4] in F minor
          1935, BBC, London – Boult
          Revised (last note of slow movt) about 1957
1938–43   Symphony [No. 5] in D major
          1943, Henry Wood Proms, London – Vaughan Williams
          Revised 1951
1944–7    Symphony [No. 6] in E minor
          1948, Royal Phil. Soc., London – Boult
          Revised (Scherzo) 1950
1949–52   *Sinfonia Antartica*
          1953, Hallé Concerts, Manchester – Barbirolli
1953–5    Symphony No. 8 in D minor
          1956, Hallé Concerts, Manchester – Barbirolli
          Revised (Finale) 1956
1956–7    Symphony No. 9 in E minor
          1958, Royal Phil. Soc., London – Sargent
          Revised 1958

Like Elgar before him, Vaughan Williams accepted the traditional plan of the symphony. Apart from the *Antartica,* which is an exception in several respects, all his symphonies are in the usual four movements. In Nos. 1-6 most movements are shaped according to some well-established principle – sonata form, shortened sonata (slow movements), scherzo and trio, etc. – but the forms are modified, increasingly, by the individuality of the thought which creates them. Take, for instance, the sonata movements: one cannot fail to be struck by the way in which convention is simultaneously challenged and upheld, observed in the letter yet contradicted in spirit – in, say, the opening movements of the *Pastoral* and the Fifth, which are lyrical expressions owing little to sonata conflict as traditionally understood. But it is in the finales that we find the most free and varied designs; and it is there, too, that Vaughan Williams has made his most personal contribution to symphonic form – the epilogue.

### THE SYMPHONIC EPILOGUE

Vaughan Williams's approach to the symphony almost always shows a marked contemplative bias – contemplative and rhetorical (rhetorical as distinct from dramatic). His thought is characterised by reflection, even rumination, or by passionate gesture. The contemplative approach has its natural, lyrical expression in the slow movements. Elsewhere it faces problems of structure and contrast and the ultimate task of providing a sense of completion and unity. The composer's natural impulse frequently led him to the quiet, reflective coda as the means of clinching a movement and giving it its final perspective: a profoundly telling example, since this is also the most truly dramatic of his first movements, is the opening *allegro* of the Fourth. Again, such physically active movements as the scherzos of the *London* and the *Pastoral* are brought to rest with hushed, reflective music which finally, and unexpectedly, modifies their total effect. The symphonic epilogue is an extension of the same technique to the concluding movement, where the task implied is that of establishing the final perspective of the whole work. This is essentially a structural task; lyrical expressiveness is not enough.

Vaughan Williams invariably found his solution in some thematic link with the first movement. The clearest precedent is at the end of Brahms's Third Symphony: the forceful first subject of the finale becomes transformed in a reflective augmentation, and the two most significant motives from the first movement quietly re-emerge. This, we are told, is an extended coda, but in effect it is an epilogue to the entire work – a Vaughan Williams epilogue, one might almost say. The essential features are already apparent as early as *A Sea Symphony*. The long finale, 'The Explorers', with its hints of Elgar and its tendency towards the big, emphatic statement, looks like ending *fortissimo* on the repeated injunction 'sail forth'. It very nearly does end at that point; but then there is a pause and a change of key – a return to the movement's original E flat – and in four pages of *molto adagio* the work is taken to a *niente* close. One of the main themes of the finale appears transformed; it is now more fragmentary and is expressively shaded by the gradual emergence of two alternating chords which quietly dominate the closing bars. There is a fleeting, but significant, reference to the principal theme of the first movement. All this is prophetic indeed.

In *A London Symphony* the epilogue emerges as an essential part of the overall design; it matches the quiet introduction, and together these two features place the 'action' of the work within a deeply contemplative frame. Much the same happens in the *Antartica*, written nearly forty years later. It is noticeable that in both these works the listener is invited by a *niente* close to reflect further on 'action' which culminates in a suffering, tragic vision: the finale of the *London*, though a flawed movement (see p. 23), impresses through the authenticity of its musical imagery, especially the harrowing, climactic imagery which recurs again and again in the later symphonies.

Ex. 1 is how we hear it at the outset. At the climax, which immediately precedes the Epilogue, the impact is maximised, and in the Epilogue itself *a* and *b* are quietly but ominously recalled, so that the warm sound of G major in the closing bars is far from wiping the slate clean. Spiritually, and perhaps musically, one catches here a distant intimation of the Epilogue of the Sixth, that desolate utterance whose importance for the composer's subsequent development may not even now have been fully appreciated.

The Epilogue of the Sixth is itself the finale, though in an unusual situation where all four movements are played without a break. In the Fifth and the Fourth it is an integral part of the finale and is felt to be the fulfilment of the whole work, both musically and spiritually; which makes impressive evidence concerning Vaughan Williams's symphonic methods, for in their tone and temper these two symphonies – the 'violent' Fourth, the 'serene' Fifth – could not be further apart. Of the first seven symphonies, only the *Pastoral* does not have an epilogue as such. But this is misleading, for the finale has its own prologue and epilogue in which a solo soprano voice sums up the modal and pentatonic outlines characteristic of the whole work, and so the function is duly discharged – to particularly beautiful effect.

The fact that the epilogue is dispensed with in the Eighth and the Ninth is one more pointer to the special interest of Vaughan Williams's final period.

## The First Three Symphonies

Each of these works marks a different stage in Vaughan Williams's grasp of symphonic expression. *A Sea Symphony* was fabricated, laboriously and over a number of years, from an assortment of ideas which the composer willed into a coherent statement. It was his first large-scale composition. That it became a symphony at all is significant, a triumph of instinct over environment. For this very ambitious score started life as 'Songs of the Sea', in emulation of Stanford; not until 1906 did Vaughan Williams begin to call it his 'Ocean Symphony' (*sic*). Even then there was a great deal of rejection and rewriting, some of it when the full score was otherwise complete. At one stage a whole movement was abandoned, though a fragment of it survives in the finale.[1]

*A London Symphony* is far more strongly constructed, yet this, too, is in some sense a fabricated work. The composer tells us that, prompted by his friend Butterworth, he looked out the music he had sketched for 'a symphonic poem [!] about London, and decided to throw it into symphonic form'. Legs are being pulled, of course, but it does not follow that the story is unfounded. The musical ideas are certainly heterogeneous, and the unity achieved is to some extent dependent on the composer's by now well-defined personality, and on his very skilful joinery. Nonetheless, the work has a momentum, a roundness, a certainty of effect that can only be thought of as symphonic.

The *London,* then, is a 'well-made' symphony. As a comment on the *Pastoral,* how patronising and inept that would seem! For the *Pastoral* is the first Vaughan Williams symphony in which means and ends are wholly attuned. Its achievement is especially remarkable on account of the music's apparent defiance of so much that

[1] The whole fascinating story is admirably documented in Michael Kennedy, *op. cit.*

makes a symphony 'go': large-scale contrast, variety of mood and tempo, tunes that the mind latches on to. Instead of these – in any obvious guise, that is – we find a rapt, brooding presence, at first hard to connect with, yet strangely compelling in its magic of sound. The oneness of the imaginative conception does not need demonstrating; it is there in the idiom, in the very idiosyncrasy of the musical thought.

Vaughan Williams's development through these first three symphonies is as much a matter of style and expression as of an increasing inwardness in handling the form. The one keeps pace with the other. In *A Sea Symphony* there is much that is Parry's or Stanford's – eloquent choralism of a somewhat conventional nobility – and more than a trace of Elgar, especially in the finale. There is much else besides, but the incongruities are inescapable. Although Vaughan Williams's most crucial formative experiences, the 'discovery' of folk-song and of Elizabethan and Jacobean music, date from this period, their transforming effect appears fitfully and inconclusively. In the *London*, however, both melody and harmony are strongly individual throughout, the one due largely to the influence of folk-song and the modes, the other to a confident juxtaposing of major and minor triads in a way that had already given Parry some misgivings.[1] This treatment of common chords was undoubtedly reinforced by the so-called 'false relations' found in the music of the Elizabethans – see, for instance, Vaughan Williams's great string piece, the Fantasia on a Theme by Thomas Tallis (1910) – but there was also a further stimulus, from a very different quarter.

In 1908, having decided that he was 'lumpy and stodgy . . . and that a little French polish would be of use', Vaughan Williams went to Paris to study with Ravel. Mainly he worked at orchestration, and his feeling for colour and texture, based hitherto on the solid Germanic principles handed on by Parry and Stanford, was given a quite new direction: something of this comes through here and there in the *Sea Symphony*, and in the *London* it is a factor in the whole realisation of the music. But his 'French fever', as he called it, did not stop there; his acquaintance with the music not only of Ravel but of Debussy greatly strengthened his instinct to move

[1] Parry declared the *Sea Symphony* 'big stuff, but full of impertinences as well as noble moments'. The 'impertinences' must surely have included some of the bold shifts of harmony.

chords freely, bodily, from point to point – what is generally called 'block chording'. And he took what he needed, without becoming a slave to anyone's mannerisms.

In the language of the *Pastoral Symphony* these elements are perfectly fused together. The style is wholly lyrical, even vocal, in feeling: fragments of modal and pentatonic melody float to and fro, turning and returning, either focusing attention on a single strand or interweaving to form a variegated texture. Block chording figures prominently too, and with greater freedom now, often 'contradicting' the tonal and harmonic implications of the melody. Thus a language emerges that is capable of many shades of expression, of great vehemence and intensity no less than reflective calm. Heseltine's crack about music for cows looking over gates is misleading: properly understood, the *Pastoral* is a tough and disturbing work, as well as a supremely beautiful one.

## A SEA SYMPHONY

He flounders about in the sea of his ideas like a vast and ungainly porpoise, with great puffing and blowing; yet in the end, after tremendous efforts and an almost heroic tenacity, there emerges . . . a real and lovable personality, unassuming, modest, and almost apologetic. *Cecil Gray*

*A Sea Symphony* begins and ends as a song, and as a song it is huge. As a symphony it shrinks in dimensions, belittled by its musical and technical immaturities. *Hubert Foss*

The remarkable thing about the *Sea Symphony* is not that it is a flawed and blemished work but that it possesses such lasting vitality. Even now in a fine performance this music can surprise its admirers. True, the worst bits are sentimental, embarrassingly allied to the minor music of the period, and there is much that is derivative or awkwardly shaped, or both. But Foss was right to use the word 'huge'. And this hugeness has, I suspect, a lot to do with the feeling that the composer, in striving to overcome immense stylistic and formal problems, is pushing himself and his singers to the limit. Which is really what Gray is saying. Such an impact, however, can never be explained in terms of noble intentions; there has to be a certain quality of achievement, a *realised* individuality.

The words are from Whitman's 'Song of the Exposition'

(beginning of movt 1), 'Sea Drift' (movts 1–3) and 'Passage to India' (finale). In Vaughan Williams's selection, only the words of the scherzo are purely descriptive; the remainder view the sea as a symbol of human endeavour or a challenge to the mind and spirit. The tone is optimistic, and Whitman's emphasis on the brotherhood of man and the unity of being comes through strongly. The setting is for soprano and baritone soloists, chorus and orchestra. Musically, there are two recurring ideas, the one harmonic – a minor chord yielding to the major chord a major third higher (Ex. 2) – the other melodic (Ex. 3 a), but these are used for their expressiveness rather than as serious structural elements. More pervasive, and more telling as a unifying force, is the melodic writing in which triplets and duplets go hand in hand. This rhythmic feature, which appears at once in Ex. 3, may have been prompted by the motion of the sea, but it is one of the composer's most deeply rooted habits, as personal to him as his signature.

The opening is superb, an image almost visual in its impact:

Ex. 2

The next two choral phrases, both to the words 'And on its limitless, heaving breast', epitomise one aspect of the work's immaturity: the strength of *a* is weakened by the all-too-easy and conventional response which is *b*:

Ex. 3

But the grandeur is powerfully sustained. At the words 'See, the steamers coming and going' a new tune appears in the bass of the orchestra, a tune which later gives rise to the most extended piece of writing in the development ('Token of all brave captains'). For this opening movement tries hard to reconcile the demands of the text with the characteristic tensions of sonata form – the tensions rather than the shape. The development begins well with the original brass motive (Ex. 2), first in C minor, then in E major, thus renewing in an unexpected way the B flat minor – D major relationship of the opening. There is no question of recapitulating either of the second-group themes, and the return of the principal theme (Ex. 3) is more in the nature of a final peroration. The quiet, visionary ending – a radiant texture created by the two soloists and the chorus, divided here into eight parts – is preceded by a very inward recollection (*p misterioso*) of the opening words, 'Behold, the sea itself'. This is in C minor and harks back, both tonally and melodically, to 'untamed as thee' at the end of the exposition: a characteristic master-stroke, profoundly affecting the D major of the peroration and the close. Notice, too, that this passage antici-pates the beginning of the slow movement, tonally and in mood. The symphonic impulse is at work here.

The form that emerges may be usefully described as panoramic (*cf.* the *Antartica*), but the tensions, the connections and the pro-pelling current are strong enough to give an authentic first-movement feeling. The most episodic part of the movement comes early on: the *allegro* ("Today a rude brief recitative') and the *andante* ('. . . a chant for the sailors of all nations') which together form the second group. However, the sectional contrasts reveal a positive response to the words and are dramatically effective. The *allegro* with its modal colouring and blunt shifts of key is one of the most 'liberated' passages in the work. Though not heard again, it does prompt the shape of the soprano soloist's 'Flaunt out O sea your separate flags of nations!' at the beginning of the development.

The slow movement, 'On the Beach at Night alone', is a song for the baritone soloist and a semi-chorus, the full chorus entering only briefly at the climax. But the most interesting things are in the orchestra: the opening, for instance, where C minor and E major (*cf.* Ex. 2) are juxtaposed in deep, quiet chords that are basic Vaughan Williams:

Ex. 4

The ending, too, is prophetic. Marked *molto tranquillo*, this recalls the salient figure from the middle section – the design is a simple A–B–A – in the purest and serenest E major; it is one of those assured simplicities such as we find in the *London* and the Fifth, the 'loss' of which is so significant in the later symphonies.

The Scherzo, in G minor, begins with a variant of the now familiar harmonic idea:

Ex. 5

$f$ Af-ter the sea - ship, af-ter the whist-ling winds,

Comparing this with Ex. 2 and Ex. 4, we see that the major chord has become the relative major – B flat, not B. Here, then, is a simple, stable relationship which the composer uses in the traditional way as the basis of a sonata structure. The big tune for the 'great vessel' – another almost visual image – is *in* B flat major: those who talk of a scherzo and trio, with this as the trio, have never really listened, for the point and purpose of the tune is not contrast but climax and fulfilment. The effect is judged exactly, and its nature is symphonic, not sectional or episodic. The tune itself both invites and defies comparison with Parry or with Elgar; it is clearly by the man who wrote *Sine nomine* ('For all the saints') and has the same broad unison quality. Notice the 'fingerprint' at the end:

Ex. 6

af - ter she pass – – – es,

Though unexpected here, this little figure with its characteristic tension is heard again and again in Vaughan Williams's symphonies.

After a short transition, which is mainly orchestral, both subjects are recapitulated in a much curtailed form, in G minor and major respectively. This is the one movement in which the words are pushed about by the music. Because the poem is loosely descriptive, lines can be detached, pieced together and repeated as the music demands. No wonder the structure is so firm. This exhilarating, extrovert piece – 'The Waves' is its title – does not attempt to rival

*La Mer* in orchestral subtlety, but its imagery is by no means stale and its vigour is infectious.

In the finale, 'The Explorers', the composer sets himself an almost impossible task. The text is not only longer than that of the other three movements put together but is also Whitman at his most giddily metaphysical. A musical setting is almost bound to seem inflated. Why, then, was it chosen? Surely the clue is in the following lines, which come towards the end:

> Reckless O Soul, exploring, I with thee, and thou with me,
> For we are bound where mariner has not yet dared to go,
> And we will risk the ship, ourselves and all.

Here the 'great vessel' of the scherzo becomes man himself, and the sea the limitless realm of his 'unsatisfied soul'. Quite apart from its intrinsic appeal, this theme has the merit of linking up with thoughts expressed in the slow movement and of raising the finale to a higher plane – theoretically, that is.

Even if the text had been more manageable, it is doubtful whether at that time Vaughan Williams was sufficiently sure of himself to succeed with such a theme. Gray's 'puffing and blowing' is apposite, and it seems significant that it is here, in this most ambitious movement, that we find the greatest stylistic confusion, including one or two barely believable sentimentalities.

The soft, unison opening (*grave e molto adagio*) arouses high expectations, especially when it follows closely upon the end of the scherzo: the secret lies in the flattened sub-mediant relationship of the new key (E flat) to the old (G). But it soon becomes apparent that there is something wrong with the expressive tone. What Vaughan Williams needed here was the language of *Job* and the Fifth Symphony; what he resorted to was an alien 'nobility' in the manner of Elgar – and he knew it. The objection is not that the music is derivative. After all, there is much elsewhere in the work that is felt to be derivative but in its context more or less right. No, the objection is that the tone is wrong: a pseudo-Elgarian solemnity is inadequate for such words as 'With inscrutable purpose, some hidden prophetic intention' (vocal score, p. 84). Almost at once the music changes: the thought of Adam and Eve and 'their myriad progeny' prompts a modal tune, processional in character and akin to Holst. This is authentic, but it gets mixed up with a crib from *Gerontius* (p. 88), and when we reach 'the prophet worthy that name' Elgar is again at hand, despite the consecutive

triads of the preceding build-up and the blunt shift of key (p. 92).
Vaughan Williams had wanted to study with Elgar but had had to
content himself with *Gerontius* and the *Enigma* in full score. It was a
move in the wrong direction and might have confused him several
years longer but for his 'discovery' of Ravel.

The many changes in style are underlined by the absence of a
coherent shape. The apologists explain that this finale is really two
movements in one, or that it leads us ever further into the unknown; but no special pleading can give it the shape it so con-
spicuously lacks. As for leading us further, is it not rather the case
that, the headier the words become, the more makeshift is the
music? But there is still the quasi-epilogue with its two alternating
chords. This image of the unknown, the infinite, is true to the
composer's deepest instinct. At the close, however, instead of
achieving his effect by harmony alone – *cf.* the end of the Sixth – he
resorts to contrasting extremes of pitch. Harmonic insecurity is at
the root of many of the work's shortcomings.

## A LONDON SYMPHONY

A better title would perhaps be 'Symphony by a Londoner'. . . . The music is
intended to be self-expressive, and must stand or fall as 'absolute' music.

                                                                        RVW

*A Sea Symphony* stands at the end of Vaughan Williams's long
apprenticeship, the *London* at the beginning of his maturity. The
dates are misleading; the crucial years for the *Sea Symphony* are
1906–8, immediately *before* the composition of *On Wenlock Edge*,
*The Wasps* and the Tallis Fantasia. So far as imagery and style are
concerned, these are the works that form the background to the
*London*. Together they may be said to represent an astonishing leap
forward, a sudden realisation of the composer's identity; without
them this first purely orchestral symphony would have been a
different work. It is the biggest work from that period – roughly
1909–14 – and also the one in which the philosophy of musical
citizenship (see p. 5) found its richest expression.

About the title: 'A London Symphony' implies some sort of
programme; 'Symphony by a Londoner' suggests specific promptings, nothing more. A couple of references to the Westminster
Chimes (Introduction and Epilogue), the jingle of hansoms and the
cry of 'sweet lavender' (slow movement), the sound of street

musicians in the Scherzo – these do not amount to a programme. If the term is to be applied with any strictness, then the *London* is no more programmatic than the *Eroica*. The fact that we go on supposing otherwise is a back-handed tribute to the work's compelling atmosphere and power of communication – in a word, its humanity. For this is large-hearted music; remarkably so, even by Vaughan Williams's standards. Often the human promptings, whether sights, sounds or thoughts, seem almost within our grasp, bringing melody, rhythm and harmony to the brink of articulate speech. But the composer's comment still holds: 'the music is intended to be self-expressive . . .'. An image remains an image, however definite the 'interpretation' one chooses to give it.

We know that the *London* was constructed, pieced together, rather than conceived organically. The same is true of a number of the world's most popular symphonies. What matters is not the means, but whether the composer has achieved a symphonic end. Do we feel that everything contributes, that the musical ideas act on one another, creating an expression that is more than the sum of its parts? The only major weakness in the *London* is in the middle of the finale; the other three movements have a conviction, a wholeness, which repeated listening does nothing to diminish. Rather the contrary, for one's first impression is likely to be dominated by the wealth of incident, whereas renewed acquaintance brings to light the inner connections. Actually, it is a work in which one goes on making new discoveries. For instance, it appears that many analysts have missed one very fine imaginative stroke. This is at the end of the Scherzo, in what is usually described as the coda, though it is more in the nature of a reflective afterthought to the coda. The main impulse of the Scherzo dies away with one repeated fragment, and dark stirrings are heard among the muted strings, first from the cellos and basses, then the violins:

Ex. 7

This 'afterthought' anticipates the wailing cry at the beginning of the finale – see Ex. 1, bars 6–10 (p. 11). Its poignancy is unexpected, yet we hear it in relation to the receding scherzo; we look backwards, not forwards. And then, when the finale begins, we feel that we have been there already but cannot account for it. The usual explanation is that the cry recalls the opening theme of the first movement, which is similarly chromatic:

Ex. 8    Allegro risoluto

No doubt there is something in that – notice how inevitable (unremarkable) it seems when the first movement is in fact recalled at the end of the finale – but Ex. 7 is closer in every sense, a palpable anticipation of the wailing cry.

Moreover, the rising semitone (D – E flat) which so arrestingly opens the finale (Ex. 1) is a vehement resumption of a detail from the Introduction (min. score, p. 5, bars 1–2), a detail which impresses at the time because it is the first hint of suffering and is momentarily dwelt upon. If you think this connection far-fetched, listen carefully to the Epilogue, which should satisfy even the most sceptical, for the rising semitone is heard again in something like its original context but in the manner first used in the finale.

These are musical realities, of concern to all of us as listeners whether we knowingly respond to them or not. But they are not necessarily symphonic realities. That will depend on the fundamental character of the whole expression. Do the musical ideas create the form, or is the form merely a framework? This is the point at which the *London* is easily underrated, mainly because it is so rich in ideas. The first movement may well seem excessively rich, and yet the more one studies it, the more one puts the emphasis on the larger issues. The sonata tensions are genuine, and there is mastery in the way the composer uses them. The structure is binary rather than ternary; the great explosion at the start of the development – Ex. 8 intensified – is the beginning of a second part in which the formal recapitulation of the first group of themes is drastically curtailed and mainly *pianissimo*. Broadly speaking, there are plenty of precedents; what is so original, and so typically Vaughan Williams, is the absorbed, lyrical nature of most of the development. The 'explosion' is still reverberating when the rising fourths of the Introduction are sounded by the horns and quietly assimilated by solo woodwinds as a prefix to some first-subject material which is now lyrically transformed:

Ex. 9

As this is spontaneously extended in a free imitative manner, the mood becomes increasingly absorbed: the treatment and the scoring foreshadow the *Pastoral Symphony*. Then comes a rapt, idyllic episode which brings the music almost to a standstill (min. score, p. 43). But even this, the most secluded of byways, is entered *and* departed from with complete security. Its innocent charm makes light of the fact that the placing of such an episode – an enclave of stillness – at the centre of the design is one of the biggest risks a sonata composer can take.[1] If there is any miscalculation in this movement, it is in the coda, which is perhaps over-conscientious in drawing together all the available threads.

The slow movement (*lento*) fulfils the orchestral promise of its forerunner in the *Sea Symphony*. Perhaps this is the place to mention the sureness and beauty of the scoring, an aspect of the *London* that is seldom sufficiently emphasised: Barbirolli's fine recording is invaluable here. For the range of expression is established as much by the contrasting colours and densities of sound as by any other means. The first theme bears a family resemblance to Ex. 9:

Ex. 10

And so we are not sure whether it really is a new theme – an experience which becomes pervasive in the *Pastoral*. This movement is both more economical and more closely knit than at first appears: much comes from Ex. 10, especially from its closing figure with the rising fourth (*b*); even the later viola theme (unaccompanied) has its origin in the previous bar (*a*).

The Scherzo, sub-titled Nocturne, is a lithe, springy movement, for the most part subdued with light, airy textures, but capable of vehemence and passion.[2] Like the perky (second-group) tune in

[1] There is another fine example (*lento*) in the finale of the Fourth Symphony.

[2] Barbirolli's slow tempo is a revelation! Surprisingly, the rhythmic qualities are strengthened and enhanced (HMV ASD 2360).

the first movement, its melodic character seems as close to street music as to folk-song. The form rejects description as 'scherzo and two trios', for the trio-like sections are really more rondo-like, so strong is the feeling of continuity and interaction.

The finale is the movement that was most drastically revised. Major cuts were made, which not only shortened it but modified the shape. This is now effectively A–B–A, with two slow march sections enclosing a central *allegro*. The march tune is deeply characteristic, and the crisis to which it is later worked brings a moving and memorable climax, the goal, as it seems, of the whole symphony. But the change to *allegro*, contrived by quickening a two-bar figure from the march, sounds forced, as indeed does the strenuous busyness of the *allegro* itself. This betrays a certain over-anxiousness, rather in the manner of the coda in the first movement, and in retrospect one questions its place in the overall scheme. Does the slow march really need such a foil? As soon as the march returns, the touch is sure again, and nowhere more so than when screwing up the climax to an almost unbearable pitch of intensity. And then, in the shadow of that climax, comes the Epilogue, turning, like the Introduction, on the harp's imitation of the Westminster Chimes.

The difference between the Introduction and the Epilogue is that between innocence and experience. Something of the 'blessed-ness' of the Introduction does at length return, as if from a very great distance, but the predominant mood is one of chastened sublimity. When Michael Kennedy asked about the 'meaning' of the Epilogue, Vaughan Williams referred him to the end of Wells's *Tono-Bungay* (first published 1909). There is much in the last chapter, 'Night and the Open Sea', that one *feels* to be not only relevant but closely bound up with the musical expression. This, for instance:

Light after light goes down. England and the Kingdom, Britain and the Empire, the old prides and the old devotions, glide abeam, astern, sink down upon the horizon, pass – pass. The river passes, London passes, England passes. . . .

The likely impact on the composer of *A Sea Symphony* – the dates are significant – does not need stressing. Whitman's 'unsatisfied soul' and the image of the sea are powerfully renewed and transformed. But it is night now; Wells's thought is sterner and more sober:

Through the confusion something drives, something that is at once human achievement and the most inhuman of all existing things . . . something we draw by pain and effort out of the heart of life, that we disentangle and make clear. . . . I see it always as austerity, as beauty. This thing we make clear is the heart of life. It is the one enduring thing.

## PASTORAL SYMPHONY

It will never be a popular work; but there will always be admirers of Vaughan Williams who find the *Pastoral* the most moving and personal of his works. In its pages, the emotions of war are recollected in tranquillity free from complacency.

*Michael Kennedy*

. . . VW rolling over and over in a ploughed field on a wet day. *Hugh Allen*

Apart from No. 9, the *Pastoral* is still the least known of Vaughan Williams's symphonies, for reasons which have everything to do with its musical character. Sibelius's comment on his own Fourth Symphony – 'by no means a concert item . . . absolutely nothing of the circus about it' – is equally appropriate here, and the textures are such that in anything less than a devoted, superlative performance the essential rapture of the music tends to be withheld.

Both the *Sea Symphony* and the *London* were written before World War I. That the *Pastoral* came after the war might reasonably be deduced from the music itself; from the expressive tone, that is. There is nothing here of that 'old-fashioned revelling in the general situation',[1] that pre-war Liberal optimism which made the *Sea Symphony* what it is and contributed to the richness and variety of its successor, despite the new note of anguish. From the 'revelling' point of view, the mood of the *Pastoral* is detached and utterly absorbed; it is suggestive of a man thrown back on his innermost resources, seeking, in Lawrence's sense, to discover the roots of his being. Kennedy's reference to the 'emotions of war' is not gratuitous. We know that ideas for the *Pastoral* – or rather, and more deeply, the Idea – began to form in the composer's mind as early as 1916, when he was in France with the RAMC.

'Pastoral' suggests landscape, and so does this symphony. To say as much is not to impute a descriptive intention but simply to recognise the music's very strong, and meaningful, associative qualities. The wealth of modal and pentatonic melody and the soft harmonic dissonances suggest an elegiac landscape; but there is also a note of visionary rapture, an intimation of a belief that is

[1] Hardy, *The Return of the Native*.

almost Wordsworthian: if the solo soprano voice in the finale does not signify some essential bond of blessedness between Man and Nature, then one might as well use the solo clarinet which is prescribed as a possible alternative; the clarinet would be less misleading.

Something has already been said of the musical means. Melodically and harmonically, the *Pastoral* renews many of the most individual features of the *London*, and renewal implies both greater concentration and greater freedom. Consider, for instance, the opening bars, in which a mood of active contemplation is created at once:

Ex. 11

Triadic block chording is not only absolute here but has an added dimension – counterpoint. The two streams of chords are quite distinct, the one on the woodwinds gently undulating, the other moving firmly with more definite intent. There is little enough give and take; the two go together but retain their separateness. The result is a characteristic rhythmic and harmonic tension. This new experience has many parallels throughout the work: in, for example, the passage (slow movement) where a natural E flat trumpet is heard against quiet chords on the strings, and at the first entry of the strings in the finale (min. score, p. 85) where the harmonies formed by the violas and cellos move downwards independently of the rising violins. There is another parallel at the beginning of the slow movement: over a held chord of F minor (muted strings) a solo horn ruminates on a pentatonic idea whose separateness is emphasised by the prominence of the notes A natural, G and E:

Ex. 12

Just before the close of this movement, two *melodies* go together on terms of complete separateness: one is a variant of Ex. 12 (clarinet), the other the E flat trumpet theme, played now on a natural horn.[1] If we are still outside the *Pastoral*, or if the players mistakenly try to accommodate each other, this passage will sound like a miscalculation, but in fact it is of the essence of the work. For it is through such tensions and the 'perspective' they create – almost literally perspective – that this predominantly slow, quiet symphony achieves its dramatic power.

The opening movement (*molto moderato*) is a beautifully accomplished sonata form, almost in spite of itself. The way in which the traditional plan, or principle of construction, is adapted to the needs of a very personal melodic style bent on 'rolling over and over', turning and returning, is of absorbing interest and repays close study. (Allen's witty remark embodies a profound insight.) This melodic style is not simply a sublimation of folk-song, although in Ex. 11, the lower line is related to folk-song. Some material carries hints of bird-song and other country sounds:

Ex. 13

Ex. 13 is the transitional theme between the two groups. Its extension by means of subtly varied imitation is another link with the *London* (first movement, development); the texture is that of orchestral chamber music with nowhere a superfluous thread. The scoring of the *Pastoral* is wonderfully sensitive and sure, an object-lesson in

[1] The composer's insistence on natural instruments (without valves) for this theme was aimed at giving the flattened seventh its true pitch.

the adjustment of means to ends. In later life Vaughan Williams often referred to what he felt was his defective technique. He meant it, but many were misled. Listen to the development in this opening movement: first, the quiet fullness at the return of the opening, now centred on A; then the extraordinary openness and clarity of the mosaic of themes which follows (min. score, pp. 14–15), and the gradual filling-in at the approach to the climax. At each stage the music and the scoring are one.

The absorbed mood of the first movement carries over into the second (*lento moderato*); even the themes – Ex. 12 is the first – bear a family resemblance. But the tone is more elegiac and the texture more continuous. Despite the quiet assurance of a familiar scene, the events of this movement are deeply disturbing. At the close the violins (*ppp*) rise high above the stave – towards what? Certainly not blessedness. One likely answer is the desolate Epilogue of the Sixth.

The third movement (*moderato pesante*) was described by the composer as a slow dance. The basic plan is that of a scherzo (G minor) with two trios (G major), but this is followed by a passage marked *presto* for which 'coda' would be woefully inadequate. One's immediate impression is of much-needed relief, for the movement begins *f molto pesante* with a firm rhythm on lower strings and horns:

Ex. 14

*f molto pesante*

But at the fourth bar the pulse is modified, and seven bars later comes a trumpet tune in cross-rhythm with the lower strings: listeners and players alike need real alertness, for this is to be no earth-bound galumphing. After the first climax we are in 'impressionist' country with a Ravel-like flute arabesque and the lightest of textures. Even the sturdy folk-song tune of the trio sections has unexpected consequences; the tone, surely, is mock-serious. The final *presto* – prompted, perhaps, by the 'afterthought' in the scherzo of the *London* (1920 version) – is like a light wind blowing in from nowhere; it picks up the first trumpet tune and, at the close, the initial rhythmic theme (Ex. 14), but is itself a new impulse, aerial and fantastic.

Thus the scherzo dissolves into thin air, in a way that makes a natural transition to the finale. This should follow after the briefest of pauses; the spell must not be broken. The distant soprano voice with which the finale begins and ends (*lento*) has already been mentioned, both as a symbol and, less controversially, as a means of enhancing what is really a summing-up of the work's most characteristic melodic expressions. The other element (*moderato maestoso*) is the most sustained song melody (woodwinds) in the entire symphony and carries with it an inescapable feeling of community. The climax of this theme, especially on its return, is a typical Vaughan Williams benediction, in the manner of the Fifth. Not that the emotional tensions have been finally resolved. Indeed, the very composure of the *maestoso* theme serves to emphasise the urgency and passion of the middle of the movement where the two themes interact – ecstatically, and yet disturbingly.

## The Middle Symphonies

Vaughan Williams did not begin sketching his Fourth Symphony until ten years after completing the *Pastoral*. This was to prove his longest gap between symphonies. During those years (1921–31) his ideas developed in several directions and found expression in a number of major compositions as well as many smaller ones. The former, with few exceptions, are works in which the intensely inward, visionary quality of the *Pastoral* received some new embodiment which extended and enriched the musical thought: *Sancta Civitas* (1923–5), *Flos Campi* (1925), *Riders to the Sea* (1925–32) and *Job* (1930) are the most important. There is another group of works, notably the Violin Concerto (1924–5) and the Piano Concerto (1926–31), in which the challenge of a new medium seems to have been the decisive factor. Each of these six works is a distinctive artistic achievement, and three of them – *Flos Campi, Riders to the Sea* and *Job* – are unqualified masterpieces whose seminal importance for the middle symphonies can hardly be exaggerated.

*Job* is peculiarly powerful in both respects and is so comprehensive in its range of expression that not only the Fourth but the Fifth and even the Sixth are felt to be indebted, utterly different from each other though these symphonies are. One reason why *Job* is so revealing and productive of so much vital imagery is that the subject involved *all* Vaughan Williams's most basic responses. And so we find that this programmatic work has the same sort of bearing on the middle symphonies as has the music for *Scott of the Antarctic* on Nos. 7–9. It does not, of course, follow that the symphonies are programmatic. They are, however, so sharply differentiated in thought and expression that their juxtaposition invites us to 'interpret', to seek an explanation outside the music itself. Here, I think, it has to be insisted that great music, however much it may reflect passing events, is fundamentally an expression of the composer's perception of reality. This should keep us from falling for the superficially attractive explanations which have dogged these symphonies, the Fourth and the Sixth especially.

## SYMPHONY NO. 4 IN F MINOR

In No. 4 the prophet sees the nature of naked violence triumphant in Europe-and in No. 6 there is similarly a prophetic warning of what will happen to man, kind if it persists in its foolish, wicked wars.                    *Frank Howes*

His own story of the genesis of his Fourth Symphony was that he had read an account of one of the 'Freak Festivals' in which a symphony, he couldn't remember who had written it, was described in some detail. . . . So, without any philosophical, prophetic, or political germ, No. 4 took its life from a paragraph in *The Times*.                    *Ursula Vaughan Williams*

To grasp the nettle: neither of these comments will do; the one gratuitously attributes a missionary intention, the other limits 'genesis' to the final prompting. That Vaughan Williams, both as man and artist, was concerned about the state of Europe goes without saying; that this concern was reflected in his Fourth Symphony seems very probable: but – and this is crucial – one cannot go further without (i) venturing beyond the demonstrable, and (ii) limiting the music's potentiality. So both comments are limiting. The composer's stories about his works should be treated with caution; but clearly, if the Fourth was in fact triggered off by that description in *The Times*, then the underlying impulse, the pressure to create, must already have been very strong indeed.

This view is supported by the work itself – its sustained intensity and the closeness of its organisation – and also by the composer's subsequent attitude towards it. His often quoted remark – 'I don't

know whether I like it, but it's what I meant' – is of more than
anecdotal interest. To suggest that he wrote the Fourth almost in
spite of himself would be to put it too strongly; but one senses that
the musical ideas so took possession of him that he became the
instrument, the vehicle, and in the process was himself 'composed
anew'. It is as if some immense pent-up energy had suddenly found
release, driving all before it, and yet engaging the composer's
fullest powers. The satanic music in *Job* is a related phenomenon,
but so, one feels, are the passionate outbursts in the *Pastoral* (movements 2 and 4) and the ultimate climax of the *London*. There are,
however, some important differences: one is that in the Fourth a
violent and passionate manner is the expressive norm; another is the
(significant) absence of what has been referred to as 'blessedness'.

Compare the opening semitonal clash with that of the finale of
the *London* (Ex. 1, p. 11). In the Fourth the clashing semitones are
quite naked and are presented with the utmost force. There are no
warm triads to absorb and mollify; simply the two notes, grinding
together under the full weight of the orchestra:

Ex. 15

The power of this opening is in its concentration, in the harnessing
of the semitones so that their pulling apart and their holding
together are inseparable, the source of an exhilarating energy.
Though centred on the home dominant (C), Ex. 15 is incipiently
bitonal: aspects of the *Pastoral* may usefully be recalled – Ex. 12,
for instance – but the difference in feeling will again be emphasised.

This symphony begins as it means to go on. Explosiveness and
tenacity, felt as complementary qualities, are inherent in the two
four-note motives which are basic to the whole work. The first
holds tenaciously to one point, the second erupts, overshooting
the octave by a semitone:

Ex. 16

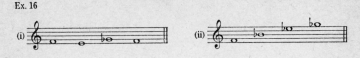

There is a comparable tension in the music's rhythmic life, between the riot of displaced accents and the underlying beat, which is regular, even primitive. And again in the relationship between form and content; for the architectural frame is strongly traditional: movts 1, 2 and 4 are sonata forms, and 3 is a clearly-defined scherzo and trio. In a masterly interpretation these contrary pulls will be not so much balanced as held in a state of deadlocked activity, like some furious but evenly-matched tug-of-war.[1]

The two basic motives unite the four movements and dominate the musical imagery. Their extreme terseness, their discordant harmonic implications and the tension resulting from their immediate juxtaposition are at the root of the music's violence. As well as appearing in their own right, Ex. 16 (i) and (ii) give rise to much of the further material – themes, rhythmic patterns, strands of counterpoint – and their importance is finally driven home in the fugal epilogue: (i) is the fugue subject, (ii) an intermittent countersubject, and bits of theme from the finale are ruthlessly enmeshed in the texture.

Every description of this symphony necessarily resorts to the vocabulary of violence. But the Fourth is not Holst's *Mars*; it is not simply an expression of violence. There are other important elements, especially in the first two movements, and these are crucial to an understanding of the work's true nature. The lyrical second subject from the first movement is of particular interest – see Ex. 17 overleaf. Note the marking '*appassionato sostenuto*' (which some conductors fail to do). Notice, too, that (i) and (ii) are not involved. Played by all the strings except the double-basses, this wonderfully flexible line is continued with great freedom and energy; each point of arrival is a springboard for the next urgent phrase, and the total effect is one of remarkable richness and resilience. There is nothing like it in any of Vaughan Williams' previous works, and it is not heard again – as a melodic style, that is – until the last phase, when it is much modified.

[1] For sheer ferocity Vaughan Williams's own performance, recorded in 1937 and now available on an LP (World Record Club SH 128), remains unsurpassed.

Ex. 17

The section marked *lento* at the end of the first movement is also revealing. This follows a highly concentrated recapitulation of the lyrical subject (Ex. 17), which has brought the movement to its ultimate climax – a superb *largamente* (pp. 25–6 in the score). The *lento* is a contemplative transformation (muted strings) of what is usually described as a continuation of the second subject, though its role is so distinct that 'third subject' seems permissible: the initial phrases are related to (i).[1] The transformation is one of the most compassionate utterances in twentieth-century music, but it is not a benediction: the chords (violas and cellos) are not 'blocked', the descending violins have an icy remoteness, there is a tonal restlessness in the hesitation between D flat and D (underlined by C in the bass throughout), and the consoling effect of the final page is that of contrary motion, not modal harmony. I can detect nothing here of the composer's religious responses.

The slow movement likewise is significant for what it is not. Despite the minatory presence of motive (ii) – at the outset and at the two climaxes – this *andante moderato* does not depict violence; neither does it offer some consoling vision, an escape to another plane. The emotional content can be discussed only in terms of an anxious, questioning humanism that refuses to be turned aside, however grim the prospect. Much of the texture is unique in Vaughan Williams's music:

[1] American readers should beware of the analysis in Elliott S. Schwartz, *The Symphonies of Ralph Vaughan Williams* (University of Massachusetts Press, 1964). To treat the third subject as the second, the second as the first, and the first as an introduction is to misunderstand the whole design.

Ex. 18

Profoundly troubled though this music is, there is an underlying calm, an immense human dignity. That some conductors seek to 'beautify' by relaxing the tempo or by pointing-up this or that detail may well be psychologically revealing – of themselves. But it is clear from the score, and from VW's own interpretation, that a strict tempo is as important here as in the scherzo or the finale.

Another major aspect of the Fourth is the composer's enthusiasm for his new materials. The very strong constructional drive is felt at every level, from the bar-to-bar working to the overall unity and consistency. In the scherzo and the finale, however, one may wonder whether an all-powerful constructional impulse has not resulted in a shift of emphasis, a blurring of the symphony's emotional unity. It is arguable that these two movements have an air of detachment, a seemingly heartless 'objectivity'. Only in the retrospective episode in the finale are the inwardness and humanity of the first two movements felt again, and since it *is* an episode the shift is underlined. Of course, the composer may have knowingly, deliberately tilted the balance, but there are two grounds – apart from one's aesthetic instinct – for keeping the question open. We know that he was dissatisfied with the finale in its original draft. In December 1933 he wrote to Holst: 'The "nice" tunes in the finale have already been replaced by better ones (at all events they are *real* ones). What I mean is that I *knew* the others were made-up stuff and these are not.' (The nature of this revision is certainly thought-provoking: are the tunes emotionally right, even now?) The second of these grounds is that remarks such as 'I don't know whether I like it' seem always to have been made immediately after a performance or rehearsal, so they may have been a reaction to the later stages of the work.

What is the tone of the finale? That it is sardonic is intimated at once, for the opening (i) is a calculated travesty of the tenderest expression in the slow movement (ii):

Ex. 19

Together with the 'oom-pah' accompaniment which follows, this suggests a parody of the triumphal march as epitomised in the finale of Beethoven's Fifth. One can hardly doubt that the Beethoven was in fact Vaughan Williams's model: the way in which the scherzo is attached to the finale – a splendid linking passage made from the two basic motives – and is even felt to precipitate the finale is not a coincidence or a subconscious prompting. And the effect is to sharpen the sardonic tone, giving it truculence and menace.

The momentum is enhanced, not impaired, by the *lento* episode which takes the place of a central development. This moment of stillness, a 'quotation' from the compassionate ending of the first movement, is a stroke of genius. Expressively, it heightens the wildness of the finale; and structurally, as a *non*-development section, it throws the whole weight of the movement on to the fugal epilogue. When the epilogue begins, the finale has already reached the peak of ferocity: what follows is a machine-like process in which the grinding semitones of the first basic motive 'grind exceeding small'.

The symphony ends with an enlargement of its opening bars. And yet, as already suggested, there is a sense in which its end is *not* in its beginning (interpreting 'beginning' as the first two movements). The music's fearless individuality and the gusto and conviction with which the logical issues are followed through are tremendously exhilarating; but the feeling remains that, emotionally and spiritually, the work is to some extent at odds with itself.

It is music imbued with what one can only call greatness of soul. If we who are younger feel that it is not altogether 'our' kind of music, we none the less respect and love it as a great English classic ... the consummation of the lifetime's work of a great and good man.                                                *Wilfrid Mellers*

When those sentences were written, in 1945, the Fifth was Vaughan Williams's most recent symphony. The implicit assumption that it would be his last was much in evidence at the time. Not only was the composer over seventy – that, perhaps, was incidental – but the symphony itself was felt to be a final resolution and synthesis, both musically and spiritually: 'greatness of soul' and purity of expression reinforced each other, and nobody doubted that the end of the finale was valedictory in tone. Today, after four more symphonies and nearly thirty years, the perspective is different: the Fifth is the climax of Vaughan Williams's development in one particular direction, the ultimate expression of his modal lyricism – and of the traditional (religious) responses inherent in that lyricism. Within those limits Mellers's tribute is richly deserved. But the synthesis achieved is selective; the Fifth makes its affirmations *in spite of* the Fourth, drawing on the 'blessedness' in *Job* – notably the Introduction, the beginning of 'Job's Dream', 'Elihu's Dance' and the music for the Sons of the Morning – and linking up with many other works, not least the Tallis Fantasia. The serenely rapturous polyphony of *Flos Campi*, especially its final number, bears closely on the Fifth – as, of course, does the composer's long preoccupation with Bunyan and *The Pilgrim's Progress*.

This last dates from at least as early as 1906, when Vaughan Williams provided the music for a dramatisation of *The Pilgrim's Progress* in Reigate Priory. Slowly, intermittently, his own dramatisation came into being.[1] Why this remained incomplete for forty years has never been explained. Nor do we know how the Fifth Symphony began to take shape, though it seems to have been prompted by some steady work on the first two acts of the Morality. The tangible 'borrowings' are as follows:

I (Preludio): the beginning of the second subject, in E major (full score, p. 7); the falling-semitone motive introduced at the end of the exposition (p. 10) and prominent in the development.

[1] Described as a Morality, *The Pilgrim's Progress* was completed in 1949 and produced at Covent Garden in 1951.

III (Romanza): the first theme (cor anglais) with its widely
spread accompanying chords (strings); a salient figure in the
woodwind arabesques which complete the basic material
(pp. 72–3).
IV (Passacaglia): the first five bars of the seven-bar ground,
together with a hint of the counter-melody (violins) and one
or two ideas for the working-out.

The Scherzo appears to be fully independent. Indeed, the important
point is not the symphony's debt to the Morality but its independent musical development; and this is the more striking in that the
same vocabulary of chords and phrases is the basis of much of both
works. The textures and rhythms, the sense of flow, the general
ethos of the music – virtually these are held in common; yet the
symphony never strays into the theatre or suggests a translatable
programme.[1]

For the moment, I propose to take the 'ethos' for granted, except
to remark that the Fifth is not *all* serenity, any more than the Fourth
is *all* violence. Musically, the essence of the work is in the symphonic evolution not only of the thematic stuff but also of mode
and key. The first movement opens and closes in a deeply modal
region with the flattened seventh, C natural, much emphasised:

Ex. 20

[1] For a fuller comparison, with music examples, see *The Musical Times*,
October 1953.

In the two themes of the finale the sevenths are consistently 'sharpened', and the symphony ends in the purest of majors.

This process of resolving the modal tensions is explored deeply in the Preludio. Look carefully at Ex. 20. The main thing to notice is that the initial chord (C, D, F sharp) is *not* a dominant seventh in G major. By assuming otherwise, many analysts have made nonsense of this opening and, not surprisingly, have missed the subtlety of the next six pages. The first eight bars of Ex. 20 are in D Mixolydian major, the ninth bar brings a change to D Dorian minor. Compare with the following:

Ex. 21

The C in the bass persists throughout the first part of the movement, but it does not remain the flattened seventh. As the music moves into F and then C (both Dorian), the continuing pedal note becomes the fifth degree and finally the tonic.

Now comes a master-stroke. Precisely at this point of fulfilment, when the tension between the bass and the upper parts has been resolved, the composer abandons his modally-inflected keys for a declared E major (p. 7). A comparable lift from the minor to the major key a major third higher is found at the beginning of the *Sea Symphony* (see Ex. 2, p. 15), only there the context is dramatic and straightforward – a brilliant opening. In the Fifth the dramatic effect is veiled by a subtle modulation, as it can afford to be: E major is heard against a background of sustained evolution in which D, F and C have been successive tonal centres, each one firmer than the last (the pedal C is progressively reconciled), but with the modality, notably the flattened seventh, emphasised throughout the thematic working. At this juncture any major key would bring a sense of release; characteristically, the one Vaughan Williams chooses is felt as an imaginative leap to a different plane of expression.

But this is still an early stage in the work; the warm, sonorous major must be limited and contained. First the E becomes minor – but with flattened seventh – and then there is a depression to C minor (p. 10); thus the whole of this E-centred passage is 'contained' by C minor – and the contrary pulls of E and C subtly reaffirm the centrality of D.

The development (*allegro*), which is less oblique than may at first appear, begins with a pentatonic string texture – *c* is the basic thread – derived from that long C pedal and its little excursions:

Ex. 22

Against the strings the woodwinds and horns insist on a plaintive falling semitone. Wind and strings develop independently: the 'magic' lies in the contrast between pentatonic innocence and an archetypal image of suffering. All the tense climaxes in this symphony are strongly modal; as the tension mounts, the modality deepens. And so it is here: the strings pick up the modal implications of the wind motive and in a Phrygian A[1] sweep towards their climax (*fff*).

Why is the climax centred on A? The answer, surprisingly enough, concerns the classical function of a development, that of restoring the home key, which is D (Mixolydian). Ex. 20 returns at once, with an inevitability that can be explained only when we notice that the Phrygian A is a form of 'dominant preparation'. This is one example – there are many others – of the way in which Vaughan Williams, in the Fifth, harnesses the modes to the structural processes of classical tonality.

Despite the relaxation in tempo and dynamics at the return of Ex. 20, the motivic tension of the development is impressively renewed in a powerful stretto on a derivative of *b* (pp. 23–4). This part of the recapitulation is highly compressed, without any movement away from D Dorian; the stretto leads directly into the second subject, *tutta forza*. What was quiet fulfilment in the exposition is here the ultimate climax. At first the key is B flat major, but after only four bars B flat yields to G (p. 25): the modulation is as subtle as the *very different* one in the exposition. After so much emphasis on D tonalities with a flattened seventh, this arrival at G major is immensely satisfying. But in relation to the symphony as a whole G is 'the path not taken': when the opening horn-call

[1] From A to A on the white notes of the piano, but with a flattened second degree (B flat, not B).

(Ex. 20, *a*) returns at the climax of the finale, the tension is resolved, not in G, but in a pure D major. Very well, then, G must not be too firmly established; so it is handled in the same way as E in the exposition. In the coda the prospect of a decisive tonality is further undermined by a hesitation between F and D (both modal). The D of the opening bars has the last word.

Nothing is more illuminating of the Fifth as a whole than an aural grasp of the processes at work in this opening movement. These are *not* technicalities; they are of the very substance of the music itself and all that is required is perceptive listening. The aim of laboriously spelling out such processes can only be realised in the listening which follows. (If you use a score, don't let the eye become a substitute for the ear.)

The other three movements are related expressions – related in their processes, as well as in innumerable turns of phrase. Somewhere in each of them is an intensification involving 'anguished' semitones – *cf.* the development in the Preludio – and in movements 3 and 4 emphasis is given to a descending, alleluia-like phrase (another archetype) which is the spiritual opposite of anguish. This phrase has already been hinted at in the Preludio (second subject). There is a further connection between movements 2 and 3: the same pattern of rising fourths initiates both the principal theme of the Scherzo and the 'alleluia' string music in the Romanza. All these connections are unobtrusive.

Structurally, the Scherzo, which is placed second, is poised elusively between rhapsody and rondo. It evolves organically from pentatonic and modal material, proves to be closely composed, and defies all attempts to reduce it to a formal pattern. In its organic waywardness and sublimation of the folk-dance, this movement is a natural successor to the scherzo from the *Pastoral*.

The Romanza likewise evolves on its own terms, though these are felt to be closely akin to the sonata principle. The basic contrast is between the static opening – solo cor anglais with strings in sixteen parts – and the mobile string texture of the 'alleluia' music. (The third element – the arabesque-like writing for woodwind – is a rhapsodic outgrowth from the latter's rising fourths.) The 'alleluias', at first muted, are stronger and fuller on each re-appearance. The marking of these passages is *un pochino più movimento*: '*movimento*', not '*mosso*', which is far more common and is in fact used elsewhere in this movement. On the basis of Vaughan

Williams's own performances, it seems clear that he was seeking to distinguish between motion and pace. An appreciable increase in pace, however slight, gives these passages a restlessness alien to their nature.

The final Passacaglia is based on two themes, of which the counter-melody is ultimately more important than the ground:

Ex. 23

Ex. 23 combines the ground with the first seven bars of the counter-melody. Both themes are flexible and capable of growth; each embraces the descending 'alleluia' figure. After ten rotations of the ground, some of which are shortened or lengthened by a bar or two, this wholly lyrical music expands more freely, though always with reference to one or other of the basic themes and often to both. There are elements of free variation and of sonata development, and the climactic return of the horn-call (full orchestra, $ff$) is thoroughly prepared through four strenuous pages. What follows is an epilogue in all but name: a serene polyphonic working of the counter-melody, a passage of some forty bars in which every tension is resolved, even that between the two themes of this movement, for the ground is only once recalled. The $pp$ close, with the strings in ten parts, ascending and descending, is pure blessedness.

The Symphony, as a work of art, more than deserved the overwhelming applause it got, but I was no more able to applaud than at the end of Tchaikovsky's *Pathétique* Symphony – less so, in fact, for this seemed to be an ultimate nihilism beyond Tchaikovsky's conceiving: every drop of blood seemed frozen in one's veins.                                                              *Deryck Cooke*

The first performance, to which Cooke is referring, was for many of us a quite shattering experience. One of the things shattered was a comfortably rounded view of the composer of the Fifth, a work that, as we have seen, was regarded as a 'consummation', musically, spiritually, philosophically. For while it was possible to feel that the Fifth had its being *in spite of* the Fourth, there was at once an awareness that the Sixth with its 'ultimate nihilism' not only negated the Fifth but *supplanted* it as a definitive statement. As one got to know the work and studied it, this impression deepened; and when *The Pilgrim's Progress* at length appeared, one felt that it was out of sequence, a reversion to an earlier phase.

The shock effect of the Sixth caused some critics to 'explain' the work by reference to the war that had recently ended – and even to interpret the Epilogue as a vision of some future nuclear catastrophe. The composer, however, publicly denied that the Sixth was a war symphony, and so the aesthetic problem raised by the Fourth was renewed – if anything in a more acute form. Why did he make those disturbing sounds? What do they signify?

It is worth noticing that the Sixth was begun only a few months after the completion of the Fifth, and perhaps even sooner: 'probably about 1944' (programme-note for the first performance) suggests that there may have been stirrings at an earlier date, and we know that the principal themes of movements 2 and 4 had their origin in music written in 1943 for the film *Flemish Farm*. The Fifth, profound and beautiful though it is, owes its purity and its single-mindedness to the suppression, not the mastery, of some of the composer's deepest responses to experience, and those responses struck back, as it were, immediately and with the greatest vehemence. We cannot know the extent to which passing events – the war, for instance – contributed to this upsurge; nor could the composer himself have told us. To probe in that direction is singularly unhelpful. The only meaningful questions are those concerned with the nature of the musical responses.

In a most thorough and penetrating analysis Deryck Cooke has shown that the Sixth is characterised by 'the persistent use, trans-ormation, and interpenetration of four of the basic terms of musical language: the minor 1–3–1 [e.g., C–E flat–C, as in the semiquaver figure in the Epilogue – Ex. 27]; the opposition of major and minor thirds [e.g., the clash between G sharp and G natural in the opening bar]; the minor 2–1 progression (with conflicts between keys separated by that interval); and the interval of the augmented fourth (with conflicts between keys separated by that interval)'.[1] These 'basic terms' are among the most intense and painful that music knows, and Vaughan Williams uses them with the utmost insistence. Such a description may suggest the world of the Fourth, but there is little of that exhilarating constructional defiance which in the Fourth both strengthens and relieves the expressive burden. Instead, the burden becomes more inexorable with each successive movement until, in the Epilogue, its insistence is all and construction irrelevant. The four movements, though quite distinct, are played without a break: the effect is to emphasise that they form a progressive and relentless sequence. The relent-lessness is important, for dependent upon it is the ability of the Epilogue, with its unrelieved *pianissimo*, to function as a finale.

The first part of the opening *allegro* introduces three of the basic terms and gives them a context of frenzied activity. (The last of the basic terms, the augmented fourth, does not make an impact until the second movement.) The listener's sensibility is assaulted directly by the terms themselves, in the raw, rather than by anything identi-fiable as a theme. When a theme emerges, this too is a concentrate of falling minor seconds and minor thirds:

Ex. 24

Even the themes of the contrasting section in 12/8, different though these are in broad effect, give prominence to the minor 1–3–1 expression. The second of these themes, which is the definitive second subject (p. 26 in the score), is an aspiring, lyrical melody in B modal-minor, later to be transformed in E major, though *still*

[1] See *The Language of Music* (Oxford, 1959), pp. 252–70.

with a 'hesitation' between the minor and major third in its cadential phrases.

Another remarkable feature of this movement is the way in which exposition and development are treated as one. Ex. 24 is really a development of the cryptic comments from the brass in the preceding bars, and the second subject is likewise exposed and developed in one continuing process.[1] In the recapitulation the contrast between the two subject-groups is maximised: the first is intensified – Ex. 24 is heard in close canonic imitation, the horns echoing the violins; the second is transformed, its lyricism deepened and enriched by unison strings and the major mode. One would never dream of analysing this movement on the lines of the Fifth; its structure is straightforward, even primitive, but well adjusted to the matter in hand, which is the exposition of two opposing forces. These do not interact; the one is frenziedly static, the other evolves – and that is all. There is something *Job*-like about the final stages, and the E major section recalls the nobility of the Fifth.

At this point the symphony has many possibilities open to it. The only hint that a warm lyrical assurance is already at an end is in the movement's closing bars, which are a forceful enlargement of bar 1 with its clashing major and minor thirds. But as soon as the doom-laden second movement (*moderato*) is under way, the course is determined. An even closer concentration on the basic terms is now evident, and the themes are united by a common tendency to hesitate between two notes a semitone apart. In the first theme, in B flat minor, this hesitation is between the major and minor second:

Ex. 25

The contrasting theme is equally baleful, with a massive hesitation between chords of F minor and E minor (brass and timpani, *ff* – p. 62). Once again Vaughan Williams rivets our attention with an imaginative use of triads, and as so often the effect is visionary.

[1] To hold that a development proper begins at fig. 9 (p. 29) is to contradict one's experience of the music.

Even if the Epilogue had been other than it is, the Sixth would still have been associated with the abyss: the spiritual desolation at the heart of this movement is as far removed from the blessedness of the Fifth as it is possible to imagine. When the first theme (Ex. 25) returns in its original B flat minor, a fearsome reiteration by trumpets and drums of the rhythmic figure *a* generates a climax which is *Job*-like in its grandeur and terror. The exclamations at the peak of the climax – *cf.* (ironically enough) 'elate above death' in the first movement of the *Sea Symphony* – anticipate the alternating chords in the Epilogue (E flat major and E minor), only here the effect is minatory and the chords (G flat major and G minor) are in different positions. Notice that the last exclamation (fig. 13, p. 77) is intensified by placing these chords in reverse order, the minor chord first.[1] After the climax this movement collapses with reminiscences of its second theme.

The first two movements are centred a tritone apart (E–B flat), and the same interval makes itself felt, both tonally and melodically, *within* the second movement. The nature of the tritone, or augmented fourth, is inherently disruptive, hence the age-old description *'diabolus in musica'*. One almost expects to see those words at the head of the Scherzo, for the tritone is now unleashed and set to do its damnedest:

Ex. 26

The first part of Ex. 26 – each stride is a tritone, each step a semitone – surges upwards with a great show of constructive

[1] This relationship first appeared, fleetingly, in *Riders to the Sea*, and not again (I think) until the music for *Flemish Farm* and the Sixth Symphony. From then on it was a key expression, and one that was never used lightly – see below

purpose, and all that comes of it (ii) is 'a trivial little tune' (VW) which is likewise constricted by the tritone. The whole point of this movement is its futile activity. The means are contrapuntal, and the method is one of structural parody and satire. The only relief, if that is the right word, is in the form of a saxophone tune, which Cooke describes exactly as 'a critical stylisation of the most depressingly moronic dance-hall music'. Later, when inflated to monstrous proportions by the whole orchestra, the tune becomes a blind, brutish march. In between, the fugue subject derived from Ex. 26 (i) is pitted against its own inversion, 'and to the delight [*sic*] of everyone including the composer the two versions fit' (VW). In fact, fitting, not fitting, half-fitting – these are all one. For the brilliance of the Scherzo is in the way in which chaos is presented within a framework of apparent order. Those who say this music 'means' war are setting their sights much too low; the vision is more generalised and more fundamental.

As in the Fourth, the Epilogue gives us the ethos of the work in its most acute form. This it does at length, and with the chilling emphasis of a dead flat *pianissimo* (*senza crescendo*). Essentially, this movement is a meditation on a single theme:

Ex. 27

Look again at the 'basic terms' identified by Cooke (p. 42). Ex. 27, which seems so nebulous, is the tightest of amalgams of three of those terms: the augmented fourth (F–B), the minor third (C–E flat–C, F–A flat–F), and the falling minor second (C–B, F–E). Moreover, as in the middle of the second movement, the tonality hesitates between E and F; and the first four notes are a lifeless paraphrase of the symphony's opening. As long ago as the *London* we saw that a Vaughan Williams epilogue could embody the subtlest of connections, so it is not surprising that in the Sixth, where a whole movement is involved, the basic material is very closely composed. And yet, this *is* a nebulous and lifeless theme; in the composer's words, it 'drifts about contrapuntally' in a quasi-fugal texture – and in the end disintegrates, leaving only the chords of E flat major and E minor (violins and violas) alternating in a void. The whole conception, including the three-fold sigh from the brass and the strings (from fig. 4, p. 148) and the oboe's more plangent threnody (pp. 150 and 158),[1] has the air of a passionless lament, infinitely remote, yet unmistakably 'the still sad music of humanity'.

This vision of the abyss is unflinching – and in its context, at the end of the symphony, absolute. Few can have been surprised when, many years later, it was revealed that Vaughan Williams had associated the Epilogue with these words from *The Tempest*:

> The cloud-capp'd towers, the gorgeous palaces,
> The solemn temples, the great globe itself,
> Yea, all which it inherit, shall dissolve,
> And, like this insubstantial pageant faded,
> Leave not a rack behind. We are such stuff
> As dreams are made on; and our little life
> Is rounded with a sleep.

(The setting of these words which Vaughan Williams made in 1950 or 1951 – see *Three Shakespeare Songs* for mixed choir – reveals a closely related response: the harmonic imagery is that of the end of the Epilogue.)

Here, then, is the 'humanist apocalypse', a perception of reality which is necessarily social as well as cosmic, and one of the root experiences of the twentieth century. After the end of the first movement, the only human positives are endurance and acceptance. It is an immensely powerful work; but for Vaughan Williams, whose music had always been humanly strong, the Sixth represented a crisis, and perhaps a far deeper one than has generally been recognised.

## The Last Three Symphonies

The symbolic figure behind the music from Vaughan Williams's last ten years is not Bunyan's Christian – or Pilgrim, as he appears in the Morality – but the explorer Scott. It was in June 1947, when the Sixth Symphony was nearing completion, that Ealing Studios asked the composer to write the music for the film *Scott of the Antarctic*. The time and the subject were peculiarly right: the

[1] The only additional material, also rich in connections.

spiritual desolation of the Sixth found its physical counterpart in the polar wastes, and the sense of challenge and endurance in the symphony was re-engaged by the story of Scott's last expedition. Even so, Vaughan Williams's very deep involvement in his Scott music calls for some further explanation. This is to be found in the music's human values and in the way these give an 'answer' to the symphony.

Now this, of course, is perilous ground. The idea of one work 'answering' another will not do at all for the purists. But Vaughan Williams was never a purist: though he objected strongly, and rightly, to narrow, limiting interpretations of his music, there can be no denying that a work like the Sixth represents a *particular* response to experience. It is equally clear that the Sixth sprang from deep down in the composer's being, and that the response which it crystallised had long been forming: one can trace this back at least as far as the Epilogue of the *London* (see p. 23). But for all its courage and imaginative power, the Sixth comes close to total despair, and from this point of view its very single-mindedness may be thought a limitation.

In the Scott music the abyss is still the ultimate reality, but human endeavour is a resounding positive, however tragic the outcome. The heroic theme which is No. 1 in the film sequences and opens the *Sinfonia Antartica* effects a synthesis of the harmonic feeling of the Sixth and the melodic aspiration of the Fifth. Each element is modified, the harmony becoming warmer, the melody heavier and more dogged:

Ex. 28

The sense in which the Scott music may be said to 'answer' the Sixth is epitomised in this first theme, which is a distinctive new creation. Harmonically, there are two arresting features· one is the chord relationship from the Epilogue of the Sixth (*b*), which has been absorbed so that it curbs but does not cripple the melodic ascent; the other is the chord relationship from the beginning of the *Sea Symphony* (*a*), which gives the melody an aspiring major third (*c*). This reconciliation of opposing forces – the 'liberating' (*a*) and the 'constricting' (*b*) – is the key to the last three symphonies.

Vaughan Williams undoubtedly realised, at an early stage, that what he was writing was no ordinary film score. All that he saw of the film was a few 'stills'; to a large extent the music grew of its own volition, guided only by the script. The idea that it might go on growing, becoming an Antarctic Symphony, was in the composer's mind by the end of 1948 and probably a good deal earlier; in the following summer the *Antartica* was begun. This five-movement work renews the 'answer' to the Sixth, giving it a coherence that is partly symphonic, partly narrative or panoramic.

The distinctive colours and textures of the Scott music have often been remarked on, usually as ends in themselves. The stimulus of an enlarged orchestral palette, and especially of percussion instruments of definite pitch – 'the 'phones and 'spiels', as Vaughan Williams called them – was certainly a strong one; but his new blend of sounds was the outward sign of much deeper changes, and these took a Scott-like imagery into subsequent works, not least the Eighth and Ninth Symphonies. The whole substance of his music was modified, so that even when colour provides no obvious clue we can tell that a piece is post-Scott. The beginning of the Ninth Symphony is a very striking example:

Ex. 29

This theme, we are told, was prompted by something in the *St Matthew Passion*; but there can be no mistaking its chastened sublimity. A comparison with Ex. 28 is revealing: the two melodies are similar in shape and motion; each is an expression of qualified aspiration. In Ex. 29, however, the 'qualifying' or curbing effect is not harmonic but a built-in feature of the theme itself – the flattened second and fifth degrees in what is nominally E minor. This tendency to flatten an ascending melody, making it more minor than minor, is very characteristic of Vaughan Williams's last years.

The unity of Nos. 7–9 is fundamentally a unity of vision, and the vision is more comprehensive than at any stage since the *London*. Each of these symphonies has its own individual identity, but in none do we feel that this depends upon the exclusion or suppression of some important facet of the composer's thought. It is, I believe, in the nature of this final synthesis that the spiritual security of the Fifth and the underlying blessedness of the *Pastoral* are no longer available. There is no contradiction here; 'no longer available' is not a euphemism for 'suppressed'. The religious response has been painfully transformed, and the music's affirmations are now wholly, as well as essentially, human.

### SINFONIA ANTARTICA

The listener carries away from a hearing of the Sinfonia an unspoken moral – the spirit of man facing fearful odds and bravely accepting his loss of the battle.

*Frank Howes*

Vaughan Williams had a lot of difficulty with this work. It would seem that there were two basic problems, one of which was concerned with the overall conception – how programmatic should it be, or how generalised? – and the other with the working-out: how to take ready-made material with its own vitality as musical imagery and create a symphonic structure and momentum.[1] The solutions necessitated compromise. It is easy to stand apart from the work and to show that it is neither symphonic enough nor programmatic enough – easy, that is, until the next hearing. For, whatever its weaknesses, the *Antartica* has a peculiar power; anyone in the least sympathetic to Vaughan Williams's musical outlook will be caught up, again and again, by the sheer magic of sound. What most reduces the symphonic stature is the blunt juxtaposing of ideas already 'fixed' in the film score: movements 1 and 4 are particularly vulnerable. But even this expedient is not entirely negative; the dramatic possibilities suggested by it left a positive mark on the structure of the Eighth (first movement) and the Ninth (second movement).

Each of the five movements has a literary superscription, the aim of which is to generalise rather than to particularise. These superscriptions are printed at the front of the score and were never

[1] For the relationship between the film music and the *Sinfonia* see A. E. F. Dickinson, *Vaughan Williams* (Faber, 1963), pp. 449–50.

intended to become a part of the performance: the continuity of the third and fourth movements is a sufficient practical reason for *not* trying to go one better than the composer, even on a record.[1]

The first movement (Prelude) is constructed very freely but falls nto three main sections. The first of these is based entirely on the opening theme (Ex. 28), which recurs in movements 4 and 5 and may be thought of as a 'motto' basic to the whole work. This is followed by a continuous chain of episodes, largely scenic in character: most of Vaughan Williams's Antarctic sounds are introduced here, and so is the other basic motive – deep bells and heavy off-beat chords. The final section begins with a 'quasi fanfare' (trumpets); the opening theme is at once resumed in a more urgent and concentrated manner, and the fanfare motive is combined with it to produce a powerful climax. The superscription, from Shelley's *Prometheus Unbound*, sums up the spirit of the *Antartica* as a whole:

> To suffer woes which hope thinks infinite,
> To forgive wrongs darker than death or night,
> To defy power which seems omnipotent,
> Neither to change, nor falter, nor repent:
> This . . . is to be
> Good, great and joyous, beautiful and free,
> This is alone life, joy, empire and victory.

The first point to make about the central episodes is that in no previous work had Vaughan Williams written so atmospherically. His nearest approach had been in *Riders to the Sea*, which is of special interest here, because the dramatic theme is essentially the same: Man versus Nature, with Man 'bravely accepting his loss of the battle'. The keening voices[2] and the wind machine and certain qualities of texture have precedents in the opera, but the *Antartica* uses a much more elaborate apparatus, and from this it derives its distinctive atmosphere. The principal elements may be isolated: the hard, icy glitter of piano and xylophone; the more silvery tone of glockenspiel and celesta; the luminous, watery quality of the vibraphone; and, of course, the more familiar atmospheric properties of harp and strings. These are used with great precision, and it is noticeable that the musical substance is invariably related,

---

[1] Record companies have found the temptation hard to resist, but there is a 'straight' performance – a very fine one – on H.M.V. ASD 2631 (London Philharmonic Orchestra/Boult).

[2] A soprano soloist and a small chorus of women's voices (SSA).

through its minor seconds and augmented fourths, to the world of the Sixth (movements 2 and 4).

The first movement, then, is in the form of a scenic panorama framed by Ex. 28: the two contending forces, Man and Nature, are thus 'exposed', and the ending is optimistic. The second movement (Scherzo) provides relief from the central issues. This begins with a fine piece of sea music, very deftly scored, and incorporated in it is a passage marked 'Whales' in the film score – hence the superscription from Psalm 104:

> There go the ships
> and there is that Leviathan
> whom thou hast made to take his pastime therein.

The sea music springs from a rhythmic and harmonic figure (i) and a related theme (ii):

Ex. 30

It is worth comparing Ex. 30 with the beginning of the Scherzo of the *Sea Symphony* (Ex. 5, p. 17): the impulse is basically the same, the main difference being that between youth and age. The second part of the movement, with its marvellously ingenuous trumpet tune, is based on 'Penguins'. The sea music returns, very briefly, by way of coda. So the shape is A–B–Coda (A), which is satisfying in itself and at the same time continues the 'panoramic' feeling already established.

The third movement (Landscape) is the one most dependent on sheer sonority. Here, too, the form might be described as panoramic, but it is a panorama with recurring features. At the outset two flutes repeatedly freeze together on a major second and muted horns intone a theme related to the Epilogue of the Sixth (*cf*. Ex. 27, p. 45):

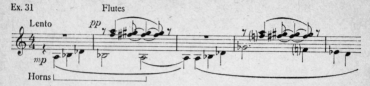

Ex. 31

The flute figure is brilliantly evocative, but the continuation of the horn theme sounds contrived, perhaps because one feels that the initial phrase should be pervasive. That Vaughan Williams used the phrase – or rather, used it again – in this scene of desolation is bound to have significance for anyone who has experienced the Sixth. The first clear landmark – a stark, canonic passage in bare octaves – consists entirely of tritones and minor seconds: the musical forces let loose in the scherzo of the Sixth are immobilised here, and the effect can be still more terrifying. These quiet octaves and their attendant theme in block chords (winds, *pp*) render the Coleridge superscription (*Hymn before Sunrise*) unexpectedly apt:

> Ye ice falls! Ye that from the mountain's brow
> Adown enormous ravines slope amain –
> Torrents, methinks, that heard a mighty voice,
> And stopped at once amid their maddest plunge!
> Motionless torrents! Silent cataracts!

After further scenic shimmerings this landmark towers over us; the organ has the block chords (*fff*) and is pitted against the orchestra with superb dramatic effect – surely the most meaningful intrusion of organ tone ever devised.

It was a stroke of genius to begin the next movement (Intermezzo) within the shadow of that awe-inspiring climax, prefaced only by a brief recollection of the muted-horn theme. Human lyricism (a solo oboe) emerges from the atmospheric terror with great poignancy – and Donne's words (*The Sun Rising*) are exactly right:

> Love, all alike, no season knows, nor clime,
> Nor hours, days, months, which are the rags of time.

The simple oboe melody seems to hark back to a much earlier Vaughan Williams, but with a difference: the many flat inflections and the restless dynamics give the music a profound disquiet. If one thinks of *The Lark Ascending* or the *London Symphony* it is with a keen awareness of the intervening years. Once more the design is a succession of connected episodes, and the looseness of the structure is emphasised rather than disguised by the brief return of the oboe melody. Both the 'motto' (Ex. 28) and the other basic motive (deep bells) are reintroduced: musically, this seems so arbitrary that one looks for possible programmatic points, but these are elusive. It is here most of all that the sympathetic listener is likely to detect some uncertainty of aim. The 'motto' is in a new form, which anticipates the square-cut, march-like version used in the finale:

Ex. 32

The finale (Epilogue) is based almost entirely on first-movement material, much modified. The main thread is provided by Ex. 32 and the tone is that of a defiant yet doom-laden march. Eventually, after a further appearance of the deep bells, the wordless voices and the wind machine are heard again – for the first time since the opening movement – and a return is made to the noble music (Ex. 28) with which the work began. This concluding section, not the finale as a whole, is the true Vaughan Williams epilogue. The manner of it invites comparison with *Job* and the *London Symphony*, though in fact it differs from both in that Ex. 28 is the principal theme of the work. Thus the epilogue (small 'e') is a fulfilment which reaffirms the human values in their weightiest and most positive expression – but also, significantly, leaves us with the abyss: the voices and the wind machine have the final say.

The superscription, from Scott's last journal, knowingly particularises:

I do not regret this journey; we took risks, we knew we took them, things have come out against us, therefore we have no cause for complaint.

This stands in place of a rather obvious and almost effusive quotation from Ecclesiasticus. Similarly, the desolate *niente* close replaces an earlier intention to end with warm G major chords (five bars after fig. 17 – p. 144). Nowhere in Vaughan Williams's work is 'the path not taken' more significant.

The symphony is scored for what is known as the 'Schubert' orchestra: with the addition of a harp. Also there is a large supply of extra percussion, including all the 'phones and 'spiels known to the composer.                    R*VW*

For the first time since the *London*, Vaughan Williams's next symphony cheerfully accepted the emotional and philosophical orientation of its immediate predecessor. 'Cheerfully' is the right word, for the Eighth, despite its many sombre hues and great sensitivity, has a comparative lightness of heart and a capacity for humour – qualities which almost certainly had a hand in getting it dubbed 'the little Eighth'. True, the scale *is* smaller, and the content does not have the visionary concentration characteristic of each of the symphonies since the *Pastoral*; but these facts should put us on our guard, especially when the first movement proves to be a remarkable set of variations embracing many facets of the composer's thought. The finale, too, is unique – a rumbustious rondo which ends *fortissimo* without the slightest hint of an epilogue.

The point about *accepting* the experience of the *Antartica* is crucial: how else can one explain the many-sidedness of the Eighth and its freedom from the pangs of a relentless spiritual questing? Acceptance does not mean complacency; the lightness of heart is shot through with sadness and anxiety, even in the finale. Much of the feeling is on the plane of warm human relationships, and the ultimate note is one of qualified optimism. The trauma of the Sixth, however, is there in the background.

When the work was new, far too much attention was given to its orchestral effects. With the exception of the tubular bells and the three tuned gongs – these last were added from *Turandot* when the score was otherwise complete – the additional instruments were carried over from the *Antartica*. Apart from the finale, however, the Eighth is essentially modest in its instrumentation. The Scherzo and Cavatina (movements 2 and 3) are limited respectively to wind and strings. Even in the Scherzo the woodwinds, horns and trumpets are only in pairs (a third bassoon is marked *ad lib.*), while in the first movement the three trombones do not enter until the final climax. There is a wide variety of textures, some of them highly transparent and dependent upon a handful of parts with a perfect balance of one. The opening bars are a striking example: consider the doubling of the vibraphone part on the upper strings (*divisi* and *pizzicato*), the delicate touches from the harp and celesta, and the melodic isolation of the flute. The total effect has been imagined precisely and is quite inseparable from the musical substance.

This opening movement (Fantasia) is a set of variations *senza tema* – 'seven variations in search of a theme' is how the composer described it. The thematic basis is, however, clear enough. First, there are two rising fourths (i), which are soon associated with the flute melody (ii), though they lend themselves equally to independent treatment. The impassioned string line (iii), with its strong descending urge and tonal restlessness, is a counter to (i):

Ex. 33

This material is used throughout as a basis for 'improvisation'[1]; the fourths are particularly fruitful, and the tension between (i) and (iii) is a continual source of vitality. Note the 'Antarctic' flattened Ds in (ii), a feature built into the harmony of the whole expression and very characteristic of Vaughan Williams's last phase.

[1] In Walton's sense – i.e., something freer than variation but closely composed.

The grouping of the variations owes something to the sonata plan: vars. 2 and 3 are parallelled by 6 and 7, and 3 and 7 bring the 'feminine' contrast traditionally associated with a second subject. Moreover, 4 and 5 are somewhat in the nature of an exploratory development. Thus the music's dramatic life exists at two distinct levels: within each variation – the recurring tension between (i) and (iii) – and in the grouping of the variations.

The range of expression is very striking. There are passages akin to the violent rhythmic and contrapuntal manner of the Fourth – vars. 2 and 6 – immediately followed by something resembling the tranquil polyphony of the Fifth, though with important differences – vars. 3 and 7. The sensuous warmth of these Fifth-like variations has little enough to do with the modes, and in tone is really quite distinct:

Ex. 34

Andante sostenuto

Ex. 34 shows the beginning of var. 3, a passage of great tenderness and intimacy in which the ascending and descending principles of (i) and (iii) are harmoniously reconciled. This variation is unique in being destined to return. The context in which the return is made is a challenging one, for the exploratory efforts of the middle of the movement have ended in chaos – a riot of disruptive tritones (var. 6). Very well, then, human lyricism must be strengthened: the scoring of var. 7 is fuller, its consolation deeper. Then a swing into D major brings a big affirmative climax: the descending chords from Ex. 34 become a broad paean; the trombones, entering now for the first time, give added weight and soon go striding forward in confident rising fourths. This big statement gradually subsides, dying away on the lower strings with a deep sense of fulfilment. The short coda resumes the practice of movements 2, 3 and 4 in the *Antartica*: the D minor opening is briefly, and poignantly, recalled.

The Scherzo in 2/4 (*allegro alla marcia*) is almost a romp, beginning and ending with a musical snook; its structure is improvisatory, each idea spontaneously prompting the next, and many of its textures have a rough, earthy humour. The key is C minor but with further flat inflections which darken and sensitise the mood, relating it to aspects of the *Antartica* and the Sixth. The contrasted, trio-like section (*andante*, 6/8) begins with mock solemnity – a piece of self-parody, if ever there was. But what sounds amusingly portentous on the lower woodwind becomes lyrically graceful when given to the flute, whose combination with oboe and clarinets creates a beautiful little pastoral episode, quite free from self-conscious 'reversion'. The highly compressed coda-cum-recapitulation – a mere thirty bars of the original *allegro* – reaffirms the basic character: the wonderfully raucous *stretto*, in which every wind-player has a go should be compared, *and* contrasted, with the fugal textures in the Fourth and the Sixth.

That the Scherzo is a new synthesis is clear enough. That the same is true of the Cavatina is, perhaps, less obvious, for nearly all the well-loved features of Vaughan Williams's string writing are there to beguile us. The one significant absentee is block chording. Various facets make this music different from so much that it superficially resembles, but by far the most important is the treatment of tonality, in particular the way in which the tonic key, E minor, interacts with remote flat keys, especially C minor and its relative major, E flat. This is an active process which gives rise to many subtleties of expression.

The contrasted section begins serenely, though with tensions in the texture, *in* E flat major; but there is no change of key signature, and the sense of the music 'resolving' in E flat is soon tempered by the quiet interpolation of E minor harmonies. Here once again, however momentarily, is a glimpse of the Sixth, which gives a new slant to the music's tonal restlessness. After a 'fantasy' middle section there is a marvellously compressed recapitulation in which the prevailing key-tensions are further heightened. And so the ultimate serenity (E major) emerges as the fruit of experience, not simply as a mood that is 'deeply felt'. That is one reason why 'nostalgic' is clumsy and inadequate as a description of the mood; another is the listener's intense realisation that this Cavatina is the music of a man in his eighties.

In the final Toccata, youth and age are one. With a nod towards Aaron Copland, Vaughan Williams might have called it 'Toccata for the Common Man': the main thematic stuff derives from the oldest and plainest of musical stock, and its presentation is generously vulgar – in the strict, almost forgotten sense of the word. However, the major-minor tension in the opening bars – 'a rather sinister exordium' is the composer's description – tells us at once that this is not a movement of mere hearty complacency:

Ex. 35

This way of qualifying D major is consistent with the use of flat inflections throughout the other three movements. If there *is* something 'sinister' about Ex. 35, this can only be in its absorption of tensions characteristic of the Sixth. The point, however, is that these tensions *are* absorbed. D major has appeared but once before in the whole work, at the climax of the first movement. There it was arrived at painfully, through quest and conflict; here it is in the nature of a reaffirmation, with the music's disruptive forces fully contained by it. (At the peak of the finale – pp. 90–91 in the score – there is more than a hint of the measured descent of Ex. 34 – in its later, climactic form, that is.) For the most part, the troubled episodes are in remote flat keys. These impinge to the last, even interrupting, and therefore emphasising, the final round of D major exultation.

The Eighth is an important point of arrival and repays close study.[1] Do not be misled by the relatively small scale or, in the Toccata, by the 'phones and 'spiels.

[1] For some further pointers, see my analysis in *Music and Letters*, xxxviii (1957), 3; a few passages have been incorporated in the present discussion.

It would be wrong to read an elegiac intent into this symphony; rather is it as if he was opening a new chapter. Vaughan Williams, eschewing sentimentality, for the last time summons up those reserves which, for want of a better word, must be called visionary. *Michael Kennedy*

It is the work, not of a tired old man, but of a very experienced one. *James Day*

This is Vaughan Williams's last major work. As we have seen, his Scott music brought together forms of imagery that hitherto had seemed to be mutually exclusive, belonging to two quite different worlds of feeling – those of the Fifth and the Sixth Symphonies. The Eighth clearly established a new synthesis, in unambiguous symphonic form; and in the Ninth, a more sombre work than its predecessor, the composer began to mine the deeper potentialities of his newly unified style. The expressive character is at once heroic and contemplative, defiant and wistfully absorbed; it is as if the human values of the *Antartica* were reconsidered, re-created, in terms of contemporary experience. There are many dark visionings, and a sense of struggle against odds is seldom far away, but the ultimate note, as in the Eighth, is one of qualified optimism.

The prevailing tone is very different from that of the Eighth, for there is nothing here that could be described as 'lightness of heart' and much that is related to the trauma of the Sixth. The composer's sketches show that the Ninth began as some sort of programme symphony about Salisbury and the surrounding countryside: the first movement was to have been 'Wessex Prelude', the last 'Landscape', and we know that Salisbury Plain, Stonehenge and Hardy's Tess were to have had some part in it. The programme, however, 'got lost on the journey – so now, oh no, we never mention it' (VW).[1] That these first intentions are reflected in the tone and substance of the Ninth is beyond dispute, and they may well have a bearing on the form of at least two of the movements. But even if nothing were known of these Wessex associations, the Ninth would still strike many listeners as Vaughan Williams in his most Hardy-like frame of mind. This is not a matter of scene-painting, which is negligible here, or of anything else picturesque; it concerns the composer's human responses, his perception of reality, and manifests itself in the very substance of his musical

[1] The programme-note for the first performance is Vaughan Williams at his most defiantly facetious.

invention. One may think, perhaps, of the sombre grandeur of *The Dynasts*, or of poems such as 'Channel Firing' and 'At a Lunar Eclipse'; it is the visionary Hardy that leaps to mind.

The orchestra required is similar to that for the *Antartica*, even to the deep bells, though without the vibraphone, piano, etc. The additional instruments are three saxophones and a flugelhorn. The latter is a brass instrument used among the cornets in brass and military bands; its tone is distinctive, and the score expressly forbids the substitution of a cornet. At the beginning and the end of the work the saxophones are treated in a way that suggests the wordless chorus in the *Antartica*. Colour is a vital part of the overall conception, though not as obviously as in the Eighth. Some passages may seem ferociously over-scored; but the effect is such that, on reflection, the sensitive listener will not doubt that an oppressive harshness is the composer's intention – as in, say, the closing stages of the Fourth. The sharp contrasts provided by textures that are open and pellucid give the sound of the Ninth a distinctive density, and in the second movement such contrasts are even a principle of construction.

None of the four movements can be referred at all simply to any of the traditional forms. Perhaps the most helpful precedent to have in mind is the scherzo of the Eighth, for while this uses the basic elements of scherzo and trio it does so in a way that transforms them, creating a structure which can be described only in its own terms. Such processes make for capriciousness as well as concentration, and both these qualities are present in the Ninth.

The opening movement (*moderato maestoso*) is not in sonata form. Sonata elements *are* involved, but the form develops freely, and cogently, from two main impulses and two subsidiary ones. At least, main and subsidiary is how they at first appear, but their subsequent activity brings about various thematic extensions and combinations which tend to alter the perspective. The first theme has already been quoted (Ex. 29, p. 48); the others, in order of appearance, may be represented as shown in Ex. 36 opposite. The common tendency of these three themes is to confine themselves closely to recurring patterns of only two or three intervals. This is matched by the imitative treatment of Ex. 29 and is one clue to the movement's intensity. Ex. 36 (i) is introduced above the counter-statement of Ex. 29, which immediately follows the 'keening' saxophones. The second main theme (ii) embraces an

ominous and well-remembered figure (*a*) from the opening bars of
the Sixth – Vaughan Williams's other E minor symphony – and
then becomes obsessed with it. This figure has already been heard
on the saxophones (full score, p. 3), whose cryptic utterance is now
extended as a new theme. Throughout this movement the themes
penetrate each other, modifying the established shapes: a new
departure, this, and a further source of intensity. The second
subsidiary theme (iii) is a pendant of (ii) and also a lyrical paraphrase of (i). At the final climax of the movement this becomes a big
exclamatory statement in C major.

In sonata terms (ii) and (iii) are a second group, but the music
does not behave in a sonata manner. The first theme (Ex. 29) at
once reappears, this time with (iii), not (i), descending above it.
At every stage some new combination, extension or interpenetration of the themes is evident – and one goes on making new
discoveries long after mastering the broad essentials. As for
tonality, this confirms that it is misleading to approach this movement with sonata preconceptions. The main tonal centres, of a fluid
and fluctuating mode, are E, G and C: these are the stabilisers, with
E minor exerting a force which in the end seems massive and
enduring. Vaughan Williams's mastery of tonality was never
greater than in his last decade, when his feeling for tonal contra-
dictions was at its richest and most penetrating. In every respect
this is a highly concentrated movement, and in its closing phase
concentration is at the service of a philosophic calm. Here one may

possibly recall the coda from the first movement of the Fifth – the tone of the coda, that is. But it is the Sixth and the *Antartica* that are inescapable.[1]

In the slow movement (*andante sostenuto*), much of which is really *moderato* ($\downarrow$ = 100), we find a reflective theme for flugelhorn bluntly juxtaposed with an aggressive and fiercely orchestrated rhythm. The theme comes from a discarded tone-poem, *The Solent*, which dates from the years of *A Sea Symphony*,[2] but the flattened Ds show that it has been re-shaped:

Ex. 37

The rhythmic idea was originally associated with the ghostly drummer of Salisbury Plain, who figured in the programme 'we never mention'. It is hard to recall another piece in which two such different ideas have been so meaningfully juxtaposed: the only link between them is slender enough – the D–D flat shape in the one, the D–C sharp in the other. The flugelhorn theme is quite static and always at the same pitch. The opposing rhythm (and tempo) becomes increasingly barbaric and expresses itself melodically in two or three obsessive shapes.

One's first reaction to the contemplative string music in the middle of the movement is that it closely resembles the contrasting section in the Cavatina of the Eighth: the key is the same (E flat)

[1] At one point in this movement–p.16, fig. 10–the five-note expression from the Epilogue of the Sixth (Ex. 27, p. 45) and also the *Antartica* (Ex. 31, p. 52) is heard again in 'Antarctic' surroundings.

[2] The beginning of the theme has been compared with the 'limitless heaving breast' motive (Ex. 3, *a* – p. 15), but there is also a suggestion of 'On the beach at night alone'.

and both melody and rhythm have a marked affinity. But the mood of this passage is still more absorbed and the harmonic texture has its own distinctive colouring. When a broader eloquence ensues, the mood remains chaste and subdued. The whole point of this very telling passage, which is briefly recalled at the end, is its detachment from the rest of the movement. Any conductor who tries to make it 'belong' is likely to achieve the opposite effect.

The Scherzo is of the violent, sardonic type, broadly comparable with that of the Sixth, though relying more on disruptive effects of colour and dynamics than on contrapuntal anarchy. Some familiar features appear at once:

Ex. 38

*p scherzando*

Note the tritones (*a*) and in the two middle bars the dual role of the note A flat (= G sharp): F minor and E major are brought together in the manner of the Sixth (*cf*. E minor and E flat major in the Epilogue).

Ex. 38 is the first of five themes. The structure is episodic and capricious, like that of the scherzo of the Eighth, only more so. Colour and texture also suggest the Eighth, and in the saxophone 'chorale' there is something of the *Antartica*. The saxophones have a leading role in this movement, and they are not used purely satirically as in *Job* and the Sixth: their chorale tune, which comes late in the proceedings, has a peculiarly moving wistfulness (block chording). Most of the material, however, is knowingly trivial, and the exaggerated rhythms are nothing if not menacing. There are glimpses of the apocalyptic terror of the Sixth, but there is also a philosophic detachment.

The finale raises problems. In the composer's words, this is 'really two movements, played without break, and connected by three short phrases which recur throughout'. It appears that this contraction of two movements was decided on at an early stage; but surely the decision was – in part, at least – one of expediency, arising from a desire to utilise sketches made for the Salisbury programme work. The first part of the movement, which is too long to be felt as introductory, is loosely episodic, and when the second part begins, it is by no means obvious that this is more than another episode. In fact, this second part is well sustained, and the affirmative climax it achieves is arrived at organically, not episodically. (The climax is in C major – *cf.* the opening movement.) But the finale as a whole is less than inevitable, no matter how one may choose to approach it.

The composer's reference to the connection provided by 'three short phrases' is a little misleading. The third of these 'phrases' is an important theme (full score, fig. 6) which has a certain kinship, both in shape and in imitative presentation, with the theme from the symphony's opening bars (Ex. 29). This is powerfully worked in the second part of the movement. The first of the connecting phrases is a haunting epigram:

Ex. 39

The way in which the answering figure (minor) is felt to modify the initial statement (major) makes Ex. 39 something like a microcosm of Vaughan Williams's final period. The remaining 'short phrase' is another chordal figure, first heard as a pendant to Ex. 39 (second appearance) but of less importance.

Despite its weaknesses as an organic form, the finale is impressive and even memorable. The symphony's range of expression is extended and made still more comprehensive, the philosophic tone is confirmed, and the listener is tantalised by a number of reminiscences, as it seems, of material from the other movements. The pastoral opening is exalted yet sadly reflective: notice the many sensitive inflections in what is nominally an expression in E minor (*cf.* Ex. 29 and its continuation). The viola theme which forms the basis of the second part (fig. 16) brings an accession of 'blessedness' – a blessedness that now is entirely of the human spirit. For there are no Golden Gates at the close of this symphony; there is only human courage and defiance of the abyss. The visionary, E major ending, with chords of F and G looming from the saxophones, is precisely that. The 'unsatisfied soul' of the *Sea Symphony* still yearns and aspires, but the frame of reference, musically and spiritually, has been transformed. Experience is all.